Alive and Writing

in NEBRASKA

LYNN HAWKINS

and

MUFFY FISHER-VRANA

Funding for this project is provided, in part, by a grant from the Nebraska Committee for the Humanities, an affiliate of the National Endowment for the Humanities, to the Nebraska Writers Guild.

First printing 1986

ISBN 0-939644-22-3

Media Production & Marketing, Inc.
2440 O Street, #202
Lincoln, Nebraska 68510

Cover designed by Marie Christian
Marie Christian's work, in her own words, "reflects impressions of my travels around the world." Marie was educated in Omaha and received her BFA in painting and printmaking at the University of Nebraska-Omaha. She has worked as a freelance and agency commercial artist and has taught extensively in Omaha area schools for 20 years. She is secretary of the Omaha Branch of the National League of American Pen Women.

CONTENTS

INTRODUCTION

Some people say you can find a writer in just about every block in Lincoln and Omaha. They congregate in every small town church, library or supermarket, increasing at twice the rate of the general population. Perhaps that's not surprising considering that Nebraska's place on the world map was assured by the great writers who grew here, authors like Willa Cather, Mari Sandoz, Wright Morris, and John Neihardt, for example.

But for such a prolific breed, writers remain amazingly invisible. In fact, most school children go through school from kindergarten to college without once meeting a real live author, notes Les Whipp, University of Nebraska-Lincoln English Professor. No wonder most kids can tell you in a word or less what an author looks like: dead. Asked to name an author, they'll say Shakespeare or Willa Cather or maybe Robert Frost.

Can a child envision becoming a writer someday without any mentors? Can Nebraskans imagine writing about the unique qualities of the state if they never read Nebraska-bred stories and poems and plays? Can we see us as the rest of the world knows us through Nebraska authors if we don't read their books ourselves?

Use *Alive and Writing in Nebraska* as your guide to learning the literate voice of our native tongue and as a resource to learn how professional writers create their works. Sample their wares here, and invite authors in your area to come be mentors for the Cathers, Sandozes, Kloefkorns, and Lees of Nebraska's future.

The book contains authors with their own books currently in print--only a tiny percentage of Nebraska writers, who are turning out magazine articles, short stories in anthologies, newspaper columns, TV scripts, stage plays, how-to booklets, county histories, self-published booklets and pamphlets, essays, journals and textbooks.

Alive and Writing in Nebraska is produced by a grant from the Nebraska Committee for the Humanities to the Nebraska Writers Guild, the official writers organization since 1925--which carries on the work of such early members as Bess Streeter Aldrich and Mari Sandoz.

ACKNOWLEDGMENTS

More than 100 members of the Nebraska Writers Guild created data for this collection. We are especially indebted to Herb Hyde, NWG president, who served as proofreader for this book, to members Catherine Kidwell, John Stevens Berry, Lois Poppe, and Opal Palmer for their assistance compiling and sending out information, to Richard Lane and Ron Schwab for financial and legal counsel, and to Marion Marsh Brown and Ruth Crone for reading the final manuscript "with fresh eyes."

Special thanks go to Richard Schanou, editor of the *Nebraska English Counselor* and to board members of the Nebraska Council of Teachers of English for their assistance, to Jerry Kromberg our editor at MPM, and especially to Bruce Dillman for editorial direction.

This project would not have been possible without the undestanding of our families and that of Bob Bruce, director of university information for UNL. Much needed computer assistance was provided by Bill Glaesemann, and Genni Rettke of Sir Speedy Printing.

This book is also endorsed by the National League of American Pen Women, Nebraska Association, a professional organization for published writers and musicians, juried artists and public speakers. Noted Omaha artist Marie Christian, a member of NLAPW, donated the cover for this book.

DEDICATION

To Les Whipp --
Who Grows Writers

From an isolated farmstead in South Dakota, Les Whipp discovered a powerful secret: " how to create my own universe!"

Physicists say there are only 11 distinct universes, he notes. "But a writer can create universes inside of universes like an almost endless three-dimensional chain of circles," Whipp said. "I can't think of anything more exciting!"

Les Whipp claims that "growing writers" is somewhat like growing tomatoes: You plant them with others of the same species, nurture them with care, protect them while they grow, give them room to sprout, and share the bounty with your friends.

He's spawned some 75 different works himself, ranging from academic opinion on *Children's Writing as Great Art* and essays on John Donne to short stories based on personal experience and lush-lined, lyrical poems.

"I found an enormous amount of encouragement from teachers," says Whipp, professor of English at the University of Nebraska-Lincoln. "I learned so much from them about myself as a writer. I stacked the deck, of course. I asked each teacher to lead the group in the most effective thing he did. Each time, I grew, too."

Through his years as director of the Nebraska Writing Project, which is sponsored by the Department of English at UNL and funded through the Cooper Foundation, Whipp personally nurtured more than 2,000 teachers-turned-writers who, in turn, took the seeds planted there to grow thousands and thousands more writers from kindergarten through college. The Project continues, now under direction of Gerry Brookes, to spawn other writing projects: the Writing and Storytelling Festivals, Young Authors conferences in public schools, and writing itself --in books such as this one, in magazines, in classrooms, and in small groups across the state who continue to meet and help each other grow.

This book is dedicated to Les Whipp and to the Nebraska Writing Project, with the hopes it will carry forth their purpose: to help new writers bloom and to provide home-grown nurturers to give them a boost along the way.

A Spring Poem

Nebraska is pregnant nine months
Of every year, pregnant with summer,
Hates being pregnant,
Hates even worse giving summer birth.
In late winter she is moody
And unbearable,
Gray as an old mare,
Is warm and cold by turns,
Forgetting her spring,
And as the term for birth nears,
She turns back again to winter, and again,
Delaying new life with snow,
Shattering her oak trees and her pines,
Breaking down her elms
Her flowering almonds
And browning the glorious buds
of her sweet magnolias.
Then she flips
To the high clean keening of the wind,
The dry pain of the prairie wind,
The screaming of the skyways,
And the hail and tornadoes
Dumping her angry debris,
Across the lives of little people.
She lurches into heat.
Summer is born again.
Nebraska lies panting in the sun,
    Swearing in a stubborn heat
    Against getting pregnant.

(From *Prairie Schooner*, 1986, Copright by Leslie Whipp. Used with permission of the author.)

JOHN STEVENS BERRY SHOOTS OUT STORIES WITH A REAL GUN

Lincoln's most famous criminal attorney John Stevens Berry will tell you he writes straight from the hip -- standing behind his desk fingering a gun (from the office firearms collection) stuck in his belt while he dictates the story out of the side of his mouth.

Writing in the midst of a busy law practice can be a problem, Berry admits. "But it has its advantages, too." In fact, it's a perfect way to write, he thinks. In a halfhour a day he can dictate 10 pages of a whodunit for his secretary to type. "At that rate," he said, "I can put out a book in 30 days!"

Although so far the middle and end of the fiction book are taking "a little longer -- I haven't been able to find that half-hour for a while," he says that he has frequently agonized for days over a single line of poetry.

"Yet, I could no more not write poems than I could not practice law," said Berry, whose traditional verse has won numerous awards from the Academy of American Poets.

"There is no inconsistency between being a lawyer and a poet or a soldier and a poet," said the prize-winning author of *Those Gallant Men: On Trial in Vietnam* .

"Both have the same purpose: to react to chaos and violence in a civilized and civilizing manner. I have a deep and abiding contempt for lawyers and doctors and other professionals who are ignorant of the humanities which give meaning and value to the profession they practice, and I have written elsewhere that such people are merely barbarians."

Berry claims to be particularly bored by adults who lose their childlike fascination with the arts and with the humanities in general.

He wrote his first poem in kindergarten in Onawa, Iowa, and won prizes in elementary, high school and college. A student of Yvor Winters, Berry won the Academy of American Poets' highest student award at Stanford University two years in a row before going to law school at Northwestern University.

He delights in a wide range of intellectual and creative activities. An investitured member of the Baker Street Irregulars, his Sherlockian writings have been published in America, Great Britain, and Japan.

Though Berry bemoans our living in a "post-literate" age, he admits giving poetry readings in "beat generation coffeehouses" such as "The Anxious Asp" and the "Co-Existence Bagel Shop" of San Francisco in the late 1950s. Most of his poems, however, assume readers have some classical literary background.

Gallant Men is an account of Berry's experiences as a military attorney in Vietnam. It includes the story of his defense for the notorious 1969 murder case in which eight members of the Green Berets were accused of murdering a double agent on CIA orders. Berry and other defense attorneys, such as F. Lee Bailey and Edward Bennett Williams, pressed for a public trial, which led the Nixon administration to drop the charges.

Many of Berry's stories these days are real life-and-death matters, non-fiction designed for a very particular audience, told to convince a jury or other high tribunal of his client's innocence.

DARKNESS OF SNOW

Darkness of snow, cold moon on rifle stock;
Heavy in lethal silence, bright with sleet,
Trees shimmer, and the stirring birds repeat
The movement of the brittle leaves. The shock
Of slow wind, edging lifelessness to me
Quickens my stare into the snow that stills
Dark forms, that may be deer, on darker hills,
Increases, till I can no longer see.

My knowledge ends with visibility!
Snow fades on flesh, crystal tenacity
Lost against heat and blindness. When I turn
It is to blindness. Other snowflakes burn
New loss against me. I remain the same
In chill monotony of change: a name.

PRAYER FOR MY CHILD

NOT YET BORN

If not the stunning grace of unicorns,
These miracles as rare. At Gia Le
A boy walks over water. Who's to say
This miracle is lessened by the horns
Of that cool water buffalo beneath?
Insistent Presence, leave him room to pray!
Yet smartly field a thunderbolt gone stray
And sometimes, at my father's grave, a wreath.

Let him move, as I move, through shatter-cane
In this Nebraska heat. Or murderous rain
In rice fields, under fire, alive and wry.
Or if a daughter, may You fortify
Her vision, that she see both truth in thorns
And loveliness, more rare than unicorns.

From *Those Gallant Men*

The actions of a man at war must be judged in terms of who that man was before he went to war; an isolated act of heroism or betrayal takes its meaning from the soldier's prior life history and the way in which that soldier, with that past, responds to a certain set of circumstances. Let there be no mistake; there is real heroism, and there is real cowardice. I have never suggested to any jury a purely mechanistic or deterministic theory of human behavior. But I did suggest, at court-martial after court-martial, that the court could not make its final judgment of the man and his actions until the jury had considered the man and his past. As to special circumstances--the members of the court were all serving in Vietnam at the time of the trials. They did not need to be informed or reminded that no word, thought, or deed in battle or under conditions of war has a precise peacetime parallel. We were all living on Mars, deceptively similar to Earth, and yet . . .

And I would walk the rear perimeters when I drew Officer of the Day and be challenged by the GI with a loaded rifle. Beyond the rear perimeter, darkness; and I would go back to the bunker and log in my tour. Sometimes I would think of my great-grandfather, John Stevens, who left his home in Virginia and fought for the Iowa infantry during the American Civil War. I would sleep in the dark, heavy room with the overhead fan moving slowly, and dream of the Montagnards with their anamistic practices, of the Bahnar who filed their teeth and wore loincloths; of the Rhade, with their sorcerers and their sacrifices of fowl. Courtrooms in homes and courtrooms in buildings that could have been homes or whorehouses, courtrooms in tents, courtrooms under thatched roofs. Dreaming--patching things together, getting ready for the trip home--dreaming of that weary land. It was a weary land. The sacred Mekong had come twenty-five hundred miles from its source in Tibet, and here we flew over scorched cathedral palms, and from a helicopter you could see the craters where the mortar shells and rockets had made the nights to shudder; year after year, a land weary with whispers and rumors, blending into the scents of a jaded weariness. The old coffin maker in his hammock outside a small village composed of nothing but straw; and water buffalo and hooches and men and women and children.

(From *Those Gallant Men*. Copyright 1984 by Presidio Press. Used with permission of the author.)

Berry portrait by Ne. ETV Network.

SUSAN STRAYER DEAL'S POETRY A COMBINATION OF TEACHING AND TALENT

Susan Deal looks for a comfortable place to sit when she writes. And usually sitting with her are her two 16-year-old cats — one a Manx, the other a Bombay.

"I can't sit at a desk—it's too stiff, too formal." She does, however, use a "special notebook. One I only use for writing."

When she isn't busy teaching English classes at UNL, or working in the university's Love Library, she writes every day. But when she works, she writes every weekend.

Deal's writing "career" is a school teacher's success story. "It's a combination of talent and teaching," she says. She began writing short fiction for classes in junior high school and continued in that genre till 10th grade, when her teachers encouraged her to try poetry because of her beautiful choice of words.

Her college degrees in English are from Kearney State (her B.A.) and UNL (her M.A.).

In 1970 I started sending poetry out, and selling to magazines" states this young poet.

"My 'big break' came in 1978 when Ahsahta Press (Boise University, Boise, ID) had a poetry contest." Ahsahta publishes western poetry. "I won, and in 1980 they published a book of my poems, *No Moving Parts.*"

"Later—and this is very unusual for Ahsahta—they asked me for another group of poems, which they published as *The Dark is a Door* in 1984."

Ahsahta is also unusual in that it pays royalties (generous ones) after a book goes into a third printing. "*No Moving Parts* is in its third printing, *Dark* is in its second."

Does poetry pay? "Usually you get paid in copies. *Dark* got picked by Anne Tyler as "Best" in a Pushcart Foundation Contest. The award there was advertising in *The New York Times* and the *Los Angeles Times* Sunday book sections.

"Poets are now getting honorariums for their readings. They're nominal," she says, "but you write poetry for the love of it."

She enters poetry contests. "It's expensive, though. There's usually a $10 entry fee. One (contest) I entered was the 'Poetry in Motion' contest in Omaha in 1985. I was one of the winners.

"One poem a month was put on the buses in Omaha. I also got $50. But the exposure was what was important."

Like most writers interviewed, Deal believes in "keeping the gears oiled. So I do write, even if I don't feel like it right now. I guess it's the discipline of the thing."

Later she said, "Sometimes the poem just happens. Sometimes you work for it and work for it."

Poets choose the perfect word: "I don't like to revise a lot. I edit—it's a kind of editing thing. If you over-revise a poem, it kills it—at least for me anyway."

Deal loves to read poetry. "John Keats, Edna St. Vincent Millay. The Romantics. More contemporary, Sylvia Plath—I like her nature themes. I like what she did with sound—not her subject matter, but how she put sound together. I don't write about the same things she does—except for nature. There's a lot of nature in my poetry. But I hope I'm not considered just a nature poet."

Her two poetry books came from living in Nebraska. "I'm a real believer in place influencing a person's work."

"Place" for Deal, was Gothenburg. "If I had grown up in the city, my work would not be the same as it is."

Deal says, "You don't necessarily need a degree to be a writer. But you DO have to read."

And, she concludes, "Just because you say you're a poet doesn't mean you are one."

The Dark is a Door

The dark is a door
you can open or a window
or a curtain that
will slide free,
letting you in.
The dark is tonight
with stars pendulous
as white buds,
bobbing and blinking on
a huge black bush,
always on the verge
of blooming open.
We go through
the dark door into
the hush and alien splendor
of grasses at night.
Of crickets whittling
away at something.
Of the cool, damp trunks
of trees. Of flowers closed
and still and dreaming
on their stalks. We do not
talk. We move carefully
into the dark. Deep to our
right and left, before and

behind, the night things are
with us, awake and watching.
In this world, something
in us aches of the familiar.
Dark, dark blood stirs.
We open the door of the dark
to enter a history, a memory.
Stones at our feet and gravel
reveal old faces. Noises
and whispers, wind in the leaves,
cries in the distance, speak
with a voice that we've heard.
We enter these nights trying
to answer. Close to a secret,
we tremble with words.
But the dark is a door we can
only voicelessly enter,
a place before the word.

From *The Dark is a Door,* Susan Strayer Deal, Ahsahta Press. Used with
permission of the author.

Sandhill Cranes

The first flock of
sandhill cranes are
a moving finger
on the horizon.
We are moving
on Interstate 80
to meet them.
Overhead the wings
are pumping like
heartbeats, heartbeats.
Opened, closing.
Closing we intersect
and split into
thousands. Everywhere
they fly and settle.
Everywhere we have
collided. We are
thousands, here and
suddenly in the dying
prairie sky. Fields
moving, fluttering
with our bodies.

From *No Moving Parts* by Susan Strayer Deal. Ahsahta Press. Used by
permission of the author.

BILL KLOEFKORN'S POETIC LIFE
WAITED YEARS TO 'GEL'

At the time, it seemed that no good could come out of playing on a high school basketball team that lost 17 games in a row, recalls State Poet William Kloefkorn. "Afterwards, the coach would always say to us that someday we'd gel."

When Kloefkorn told his tale of woe 25 years later to Gary Gilmer, a poet visiting the classroom, Gilmer said, "Maybe you will yet."

"That sort of blew my mind!" Kloefkorn recalls from his spacious, book-lined office at Nebraska Wesleyan University. "Until then I'd only looked at that losing team in one way. For years, it never occurred to me that anybody since Robert Frost had even written a poem."

Gilmer's poem "First Practice" was the poem "I had been waiting to write all my life," Kloefkorn recalls. "That was about real life."

"Waiting to Gel" was Kloefkorn's very first poem at age 37. Then came 14 books in 15 years and the state's highest honor--becoming the official Nebraska State Poet in 1982.

Until then, Kloefkorn had gone from college at Emporia State College in Kansas, where he switched his "major" from football to English and journalism, "because football wasn't much fun." He became editor of the student paper, but decided "deadlines were a pain in the posterior," and switched to fiction.

By the time he finished a stint in the Marine Corps during the Korean conflict, he was married and a father. He taught high school for a year in Ellenwood, Kansas, then entered grad school to write serious fiction--novels and short stories.

"I never felt any of those were worth publishing," he said. "I sent a novel out to Macmillan. When they requested extensive revisions, I just forgot it. By that time I had three children to support, and no time or energy to do the revisions."

He had abandoned journalism, short stories, novels, essays--everything except dreams about writing something.

Once he discovered poetry, however, the world changed." I sort of made a commitment to work writing something every day," Kloefkorn said. "With poetry, it's been an easy promise to keep."

From *Collecting for the Wichita Beacon*

Cornsilk

--For Alva Foil Baker

My wife's father is about to be buried.
The minister is saying something
rapidly becoming final.
Under the edge of the canopy,
canopy bluer far than any Kansas sky's blue,
I hold my grandson of almost sixteen months.
A steady southern breeze upblows his hair,
cornsilk of the very highest order

suspended, and I turn us slowly clockwise
because I am playing the game called
viewing the world through the upblown suspended
cornsilk hair of my grandson: O
cornsilk the Chinese elm and the wide green catalpa,
cornsilk the red earth fresh from plowing,
cornsilk the high August sun, the western horizon,
cornsilk the buffalo grass and the near nervous

cornsilk sweep of the kingbird,
and under the spray of red carnations
cornsilk the mind's last memory of my wife's father,
all the days of his life recounted
as if strands of cornsilk
moving light and eternal
in a warm fixed partial
hour of wind.

From *Houses and Beyond*

Franklin Walked Off The Deep End

Franklin walked off the deep end
of the front porch
and rearranged his head,
and the swelling was like a disease,
the neighbor kid said,
and contagious:
and sure enough,
it was mother who caught it,
her stomach becoming so round
that, sitting,
she used it as a table
to snap the beans on.
Then one evening she hurried away,

16

returning several days later,
and very strangely cured.
What she had with her
she called *Janet*,
and I looked at it
and touched it,
and that night
I tried to tell my brother
either to watch his step
or stay away
from the front porch
altogether.

From *Alvin Turner as Farmer*

This morning I am dizzy
With the plump brown evidence of fall.
The granary is full.
The bucket at the cistern glints its use.
The baby is solid as a tractor lug.
In the kitchen
Martha glows fuller than her cookstove's fire.
I want a dozen pancakes,
Ma'am,
A ton of sausage,
Half a crate of eggs,
Some oatmeal and a loaf of toast.
Feed me,
Woman,
Then kindly step back!
I intend to do some pretty damn fancy whistling
While I slop the hogs.

Trading Comic Books

Tub Schmidt is a tub because
he eats too much,
and he eats too much because
he has too much to eat,
and he has too much to eat because
he has too much money,
yet he believes that someone
as beautiful as Wonder Woman
might one day jump right off the page
and pay him some attention,
so when we trade comic books
I save my Wonder Woman
until the last,
until Tub Schmidt begins to plead, then drool,
which means that for one Wonder Woman

I can expect to receive
a Submariner,
a Torch and a Toro,
a Batman and a Robin,
a Captain Marvel and a Superman,
plus all of Tub's loose change,
and just because he honestly believes
that someone as lovely and as trim
as Wonder Woman could care
for such a slob, who has
acne, too, like him.

From **A Life Like Mine**

October

Above the linden
a full moon rises,
impatient to join in.

A composting of yellow leaves
sweetens the front lawn:
where were you when I needed
a girl to grow old with?

Tonight the movie
is a rerun of sumac,
its blue blood thinning.

No use trying to rub
the salt from the popcorn
from your chockecherry lips.
It's there, thank the stars,
for the duration.

Now frost on all the windows
is denying the envious eyes
of the riff-raff. Sure,
you may sit as close
as you like. Before the month is out
I'll say it: I love you so much
it's scary. So

you mind if I call you pumpkin?

(From *A Life Like Mine* with permission of the author)

MONEY A 'CORRUPTING INFLUENCE' ON WRITING GOOD POETRY

In high school, Ted Kooser recalls, he was "skinny, awkward, shy, and never much of an athlete. Poetry writing seemed a good way to get girls," he said. "It worked." He labeled himself a poet and girls swarmed like bees to pollen.

Back then, in Ames, Iowa, he wrote ballads, the Robert Service kind of poems he had begun in fourth grade when a teacher first praised his writing. His parents belonged to a play-reading group and would read poems aloud. With his parents' support of the arts and the encouragement of his composition teacher, Kooser decided as a college freshman to become a "writer for life."His first poems were published while he was still an undergraduate.

The reputation of Karl Shapiro as author and editor of the *Prairie Schooner* literary quarterly brought Kooser to the University of Nebraska for graduate school in English as a reading assistant.

Yet he had a practical sense, he said, "and the notion that money was a corrupting influence on writing good poetry." He quit graduate school to take a job with an insurance company, then took one course at a time for several years, all the time writing and publishing, getting into better and better magazines.

His verse has appeared in *The New Yorker, The Nation, The North American Poetry Review*, and *Prairie Schooner*, for example.

By the time he earned his M.A. in English at UNL, he had earned a national reputation as a poet--and had become vice president of Lincoln Benefit Life Insurance Co.

The company donated Kooser's time so he could teach a Poets and Storytellers workshop for aspiring UNL writers last summer. He serves on the Nebraska Council of Arts and has worked as an artist in the schools, teaching poetry writing to children.

From his glass cubicled office on the top floor of the insurance company downtown, just under the big clock, Kooser admits he writes less himself these days.

He serves as editor and publisher of Windflower Press, a one-man concern which specializes in contemporary poetry, including two literary magazines, *The Salt Creek Reader* (1967-1975) and *The Blue Hotel* (1980-1981). One of his two anthologies, *The Windflower Home Almanac of Poetry*, was listed by *Library Journal* as being among the best books from small presses. The second, *17 Danish Poets in Translation*, has received international acclaim.

Kooser's book, *Sure Signs*, published by University of Nebraska Press in 1980, was featured on National Public Radio's "All Things Considered." The same collection was awarded The Society for Midlands Authors prize for the best book of poetry for the year.

Kooser gives readings across the nation and shows his paintings and drawings in a number of collections. He does all the cover designs for Windflower Press books and has created many covers for *Prairie Schooner*.

Success may have slowed down his writing a bit, Kooser admits.

"I'm envious of guys like Don Hall who can put out a really good poetry book every ten years," he said. "I think we all believe that our next poem is the best one."

THE GIANT SLIDE

Beside the highway, the Giant Slide
with its rusty undulations lifts
out of the weeds. It hasn't been used
for a generation. The ticket booth
tilts to that side where the nickels shifted
over the years. A chain link fence keeps out
the children and drunks. Blue morning glories
climb halfway up the stairs, bright clusters
of laughter. Call it a passing fancy,
this slide that nobody slides down now.
Those screams have all gone east
on a wind that will never stop blowing
down from the Rockies and over the plains,
where things catch on for a little while,
bright leaves in a fence, and then are gone.

AT NIGHTFALL

In feathers the color of dusk, a swallow,
up under the shadowy eaves of the barn,
weaves now, with skillful beak and chitter,
one bright white feather into her nest
to guide her flight home in the darkness.
It has taken a hundred thousand years
for a bird to learn this one trick with a feather,
a simple thing. And the world is alive
with such innocent progress. But to what
safe place shall any of us return
in the last smoky nightfall,
when we in our madness have put the torch
to the hope in every nest and feather?

(Reprinted from *One World at a Time,* Pittsburgh, PA, University of Pittsburgh by permission of the author.)

ON THE WAY TO THE DENTIST KUZMA 'BROKE FREE'

Greg Kuzma planned to become a dentist.

"My father worked hard in the mill, and said it wasn't a wonderful thing to do," recalls Greg Kuzma. "My mother wanted me to rise above it."

But in the midst of pre-med courses at Syracuse University, Kuzma discovered an "emotional sustenance from writing--a way to take a moment away from the world, to look upon it from a distance and to re-cast it." The sustenance was poetry--20 published books in 15 years.

The timing was right, Kuzma said. "Things had already started to turn. Poets had broken free of the old forms, and my stuff seemed to be very fashionable. I was hired as a poet. I felt driven to write. I became comfortable. I didn't ask myself any questions."

Self-portraits, like so much good poetry, his work reflects a sense of humor with a sense of incredible awe at the beauty and pain of his experienced universe.

Kuzma's work after 1977 is dramatically different.

Before then, the year his brother died in an accident, "I used to be a writer who believed in the muse or coffee or something," he reflects. It was as if for years I had written as a spoiled child with enough money and time to pretend to know things."

Then, "suddenly I became a writer with a burden," he said, "writing out of vulnerability. My range was narrowed by 99 percent. For five years after my brother's death, I wrote about nothing else. I ask myself what I should be and should know."

At the same time, Kuzma says he has become obsessed with quality, no longer wasting time with things that he sees as flippant. Along with his own books, Kuzma has edited an anthology dedicated to his brother, called *Poems for the Dead*.

He lives in Crete with his wife, two children, and five cats. In the basement he prints the poetry magazine, *Pebble*, and the Best Cellar Press pamphlet series. He teaches creative writing in the English Department of the University of Nebraska-Lincoln.

These days Kuzma says he's writing more book reviews than poems for national magazines, returning in kind the critique and guidance of teachers and poets who have been his personal mentors.

"This work comes mostly out of a sense of guilt," Kuzma said. "After all, if it hadn't been for them, I would be a dentist."

THE MAN
WHO COLLECTED POEMS

This morning a poem hung
like a bat
from the underside
of the roof.
I had never seen a poem in daylight.
Then it flew away.
I had never seen a poem flying.
So I looked for others.

And there was one behind
the front seat.
Crouched like a robber.
I reprimanded it for what
I thought was bad for it.
It became a close friend.

Another I was lucky enough
to see crossing
the moon.
It was a big brown one
with lightning wings.
It would never have fit
in my anthology.

All of the others
I have found
while hunting for other things.
A druggist gave me one
to cure my canker sores.
A lady gave me one
she called a cat.
One was thrown to me
from a passing car.

I have had them so long
I do not notice their weight.
I carry them around
wherever I go.
I have begun, out of habit,
to call them my poems.

GOOD NIGHT

For the driver of the car
as it begins to turn
over and over
temporarily undamaged
the windshield still
an egg of clear glass
the doors unpopped
or jammed
still spinning
its force directed
at some distant farmhouse
wrapped in lights
its tires screaming
as if the road
were hard beneath them
and not starlight
the world
for all intents
and purposes
has ended--
one out of a
thousand maybe
survives at 85
end over end
tumble into a stone wall.
Inside, however, at the
wheel, a man
tugs and strains
the vector of his brains
intent on
straightening the road
turning the light
back on
walking away
and drunkenly
if it must be drunkenly
telling Mary who is
waiting up
of peace at her touch
and how he did not want
to die.

(From *Good News*, Viking Press. Copyright 1973. Used with permission of the author.)

THE ADIRONDACKS

1 Cheney Pond

This glittering's
a pond
upon which the wind
is beginning to cast
its whisper

beside it
to the left
the single blood eye
of the fire

the air is
voices
and the buzz of
bugs

deep in the
dark trees
owls call out
the mice

pillows of rocks
a soft gray
under the moon's
attention
like poems

(From *The Adirondacks.* Bear Claw Press. Copyright 1978. Used with permission of the author.)

Greg Kuzma photo by Jackie Kuzma.

HILDA RAZ WON EARLY AND LATE ACCLAIM

At a time when language is becoming as androgenous as "Help Wanted" ads in newspapers, Hilda Raz seeks out those elements and issues which make women's writing special.

Speaking as a woman for recognition of women's voice and identity is both an intellectual pursuit, as author of a chapter on feminist poetry in a new book on twentieth century American literature, and as poetry editor of one of the most prestigious literary journals in the country, the *Prairie Schooner*.

When she began writing poetry herself, as a teenager at Boston University, women poets were seldom recognized by the male critics,Raz recalls.

She was 18 when she auditioned and won a spot in a seminar to study with the famous poet Robert Lowell. She said she whispered in class.

She doesn't whisper any more. Today it is Raz's voice that sets the pace, her judgment that decides the merits. Thousands of men and women poets annually submit their work to *Prairie Schooner*. The competition is so intense that 99 of every 100 manuscripts are rejected.

Poems come in from many countries; the circulation of the quarterly reaches four continents. And like the journal she has been helping to edit for the past 15 years, Hilda Raz has become well known in the world of poetry.

Her own work has appeared in more than 34 different publications, and she has just completed a book of her own poetry. She has served as an editor and scholar at Breadloaf Writers' Conference, is on the board of the Associated Writing Programs, and has worked as an artist in the schools.

Raz reminds her listeners, poetry is "at best considered a marginal matter in our society."

As a young mother of two, she began working professionally in poetry as a reader for the *Schooner*, gradually moving to a full-time editorial job. But even after 17 years of reading a hundred poems a week, she finds poetry exciting.

"I feel the same pleasure in a good poem that I felt when I was a child discovering a wonderful secret in something I read," she said. "My perspective has changed radically over the years, however. I look for different things. And I know more."

Father

is never home but she loves him--
adores him, really and so does Mom:
his big, burly body, his flannel shirts,
woolens over interesting scars
with stories to tell. Oh, he is a raconteur
with racks of bottles in the fragrant breakfront.

He tells her not to talk so much.
His talk holds the world intact;
when it stops, the key piece
drops out the bottom and the whole
plastic globe fragments. Nothing's
the same ever again.

The size of him! The size of them all,
uncles, cousins, the brothers:
wide shoulders jutting through cigar smoke
in the breakfast nook. The deep black
marks of their synthetic heels never quite scrub out.

Under the huge dining table,
under the carpet where his big feet lay,
is a bell. When he pushes it with his shoe
an aunt, or mother, or a maid
brings out another dish
from the steaming kitchen.

But he paid for it, paid for it all,
sweaters, teak-tables with brass inlay,
steaks, furs, wicks for the memorial
candles, silk stockings, full tin box
the color of sky, plants
and their white rings on the mahogany,
and the cars, deep greens, metallic,
and the cashmere lap-robes,
and the aunts and out-of-work uncles.

He was best loved, best beloved-in the family,
whose very shadow, even absent,
absorbed all color, sucked short
the seasons, colored grey
even the lavish lilacs of that northern city

she never visits. She sends money
to an old woman who tends the graves,
sends money when the pencilled bills come in.

Diction

"God is in the details,"
I tell the kids
in the public school
at Milligan, Nebraska.
They wonder what I mean.
I tell them to look
out the window
at the spring fields
the mud coming up
just to the knee
of the small pig
in the far pasture.
They tell me
its not a knee
but a hock
and I hadn't ought
to say things I know
nothing about. I say
the light on the mud
is pure chalcedony.
They say the mud
killed two cows
over the weekend.
I tell them the pig
is alive and the spring
trees are standing in a green haze.
They tell me school is out
in a week and they have to plant.
The grain elevator at the end
of main street stretches out
her blue arms. The kids say chutes.

From Judith Sornberger's *All My Grandmothers Could Sing*

SCHANOU TEACHES STUDENTS
TO WATCH OUT FOR LIFE

Dick Schanou has not written all of his life. He did not start in grade school. He started writing in 1983 as the result of the Nebraska Writing Project, a writing program he found so interesting he repeated it the following year.

Schanou has taught senior high school English at Aurora since 1962. Since taking the Nebraska Writing Project, he has changed his teaching style. "I write with my classes now," he says. "Whatever their assignment is, I write it too, and share with them"

For Schanou, writing is meant to be shared. The publishing and selling of the writing is not the important thing to him. It's the sharing.

Shanou writes mostly poetry. He has had poems published in *Plains Songs.* His poems are "mostly about my early life on a farm near Shelton. About going to country school." He writes contemporary poetry only when he's upset about something.

Schanou graduated from Hastings College, then got his master's degree at UNL.

Each year his students edit and publish a very professional 60-page magazine, *The M Street Odyssey,* which includes all the arts.

Schanou wants to "show (students) that writing is not a hard, mysterious thing. It's not painful. It can be self-satisfying. It can bring joy. Everyone should write."

Schanou also edits *The Nebraska English Counselor*, a highly acclaimed publication that goes to all high school English teachers in Nebraska. Some of his poems have appeared in this publication.

Schanou, who is also Aurora's drama coach, wants his students to observe life and to write about it. He has taught writing classes through Southeast Community College in addition to his high school classes. He teaches students to write about things in their own past and things other people will be interested in.

Mostly writers write something they want to write. "But sometimes," says Schanou, "you write something because someone tells you to write it."

After the Pep Rally

The janitor enters quietly.
Generally we speak . . .
About the weather.

It's after four.
I don't have to be here.
He leaves after
A quick once-over.

I lug writing ideas
Into outer warmth
I hadn't noticed in the classroom.

I walk under dead
December trees.

My neighbor
Gives me a ride.
He kids about golf,
Lawn mowing.

I smile and
Think snow.

My poems are in the mailbox,
Even the one about
Snow swirling
Over neighbor roofs
Dumping on my driveway.

Things come full circle.

"Money problems,"
Says the editor,
"Lack of interest."

I lie on the couch,
Stare at the ceiling,
Think of others,
Of the fat girl poem,
Of the sad boy story,
And of the essay on tolerance . . .

My neighbor
And the janitor
Would have liked them.

I try not to think
About Monday.

To A Student

Your eyes
Your sneer
Your slouch
All your demeanor
Vociferously states
Your critical judgment:
"Crap!"

Sown seeds
Sprout and
Poke through
Rotting manure.

The essence of floral bouquet
Blown by night winds
Over the surface stench
Moves like a ghost,
A cloud in the darkness
Dimly awaiting
The possibility
Of some obscure
Dawning.

But
Few flowers grow
Amid mindless bustlings--
Bells, ballgames
And other banalities--
Presumptuous priorities
Dictated to fill
The slots of time
And kill
The independent
Mind.

You're being suckered.
But then,
As you say,
You're having
Fun.

ROY SCHEELE FINDS WRITING IS LIKE 'AUTO-INTOXICATION'

Writing poems is a lot like being up on a tightrope, claims Roy Scheele. "It's really exciting, but with a poem's mechanical needs, when it fails, everybody sees you fall in mid-air.

So far, the rarified atmosphere has kept Scheele in top form, turning out work acclaimed by such famous writers as the late Robert Frost, John Ciardi, and John Fredrich Nims. He once sat on a raft with *Advise and Consent* author Allen Drury .

Karl Shapiro encouraged Scheele to get scholarships to the Rocky Mountain Writers and Breadloaf Conferences, which he won.

By age 18, the Lincoln High graduate had published his first collection of poems, *A Winter Garden.* As an under-graduate at the University of Nebraska-Lincoln, Scheele won top prizes in the Ione Gardner Noyes poetry contest—even though he was majoring in classical Greek and working full-time as a journalist, reporting for the *Lincoln Journal.*

The need to write poems continued, even though Scheele's career took a different turn. He taught at UNL, Creighton, the University of Tennessee and in a gymnasium in West Germany. He currently teaches International Studies at Doane College in Crete. He had published three more books of poetry by the time he won the John G. Neihardt nationwide poetry competition in 1983.

Twenty-five years after his first book was published, Scheele still finds that the act of writing poetry is a "species of auto-intoxication. Once it's done, I am almost drunk with the joy of creation." But he holds off reading it for a second time as long as he can—usually the next morning. "The morning-after reading is hang-over time," he admits. Revisions happen after a couple of days, but must be done in a week, he says. "Otherwise, the feeling of a poem goes by. It becomes hard to fit back into the tone of a poem too long afterwards."

He continues as a poet because "it is such a vital art," Scheele says. "When it works, it's just like plugging into the universe. You feel a tremendous energy and exhilaration. And, of course, you keep hoping that this is the time your poem knocks everybody's socks off!"

FLOATING ON MY BACK IN THE LATE AFTERNOON

Blue above me,
a stretch of blue
clear as a membrane,
touched by the tips
of two white pines.

A cloud starts across, slipping out from
the upper branches
like shifting snow.
It's full of wet light.

There is a breeze,
I can feel it
on face and hair,
see it in the leaves—
but water alone

has my ear.
It's a gurgling,
an undersound,
like the lapping of a drain.

In what is left
of the light down here,
the sculling coins
wash up over
the pool's edge,

the children splash
and dive; a ball
floats by. I drift
like someone pointing out
the sky.

(from *Pointing Out the Sky.* Sandhills Press, Inc. Copyright 1985. Used with permission of the author.)

Scheele photo by Judy Seward.

DON WELCH WROTE OUT OF
HIS 'HURLY BURLY' LIFE

He was 42 years old, coaching the high school varsity squad and the father of three young children when Don Welch decided "life was hurly burly--I might as well write."

With only small snatches of time to get words down, Welch says he never considered anything but poetry. In the first two years alone, he produced more than 100 poems.

"In '73 and '74 it was as if some kind of giant poetic egg was hatching in Nebraska," Welch says. That's when poets Bill Kloefkorn, Greg Kuzma, Ted Kooser and Roy Scheele began producing exceptional Nebraska poetry, when Hilda Raz became poetry editor of the *Prairie Schooner.*

The emergence was heralded by a stunned director of the National Endowment of the Arts speaking at a national meeting, Welch recalls. "No one could explain the phenomenon or what was in the air," he said.

His first chapbook, *Dead Horse Table,* "purged all repressions about writing," he said. For the next 10 years he traded coaching for a job as poet in the schools through the Nebraska Arts Council program. An anthology of school children's poems is in the works.

For years, he wrote poems for six or seven hours a day, Welch said. "Now I more or less wait around until something hits," which translates into one or two hours a day writing. Each poem is worked through a number of drafts between his writing classes at Kearney State College.

He describes a good male poet as "sensitive enough to know what's going on in the kitchen and powerful enough to demonstrate that poetry is not a bunch of sissified junk."

Writing poetry has changed his life, Welch admits. "I know myself in ways I probably couldn't have if I hadn't become a poet--so much knowledge emerges as I write. If I hadn't become a poet, I would have lived by certain values," he said. "But my own values became better known once I busted my head writing them down."

THE KEEPER OF MINIATURE DEER

The keeper of miniature deer
was an old man with stiff knees.
He had the straight eyes of a child,
he walked the emperor's grounds
speaking to the white swans
and the empress's pheasants.
In the compound of red deer,

among the musk and estrus,
he was especially fond of two old ones
born joined at the shoulders,
a stag with its rack huge and carbuncular
spreading out over a doe,
the old doe with eyes like fitful oil
over water. And he who knew nothing
of life after death, who lived
only to serve the miniature deer,
let them eat from his hands,
holding out salt in one,
in the other, grain,
softly calling their names,
saying *Mother* and *Father.*

THREE SMALL LETTERS TO THE COAST

You wander in your garden.
I know that you miss something.
      J. L. Borges

1.

This morning I think of the margins
Thoreau loved to write about,
the beaches of his pond,
the broad spaces between the lives
of meditative men,
and I look up at this vast Nebraska sky,
cobalt, high, in and for itself
unanswerable. I'm fixing fence again.
Up there in that intense blue iris without
a pupil, that unfocused universe,
there is a vibrancy loose,
pulling at our lives.
Trees lean into it,
no known quantity measures it,
I backswing my hammer into this blue.
And well-water, stone jug, staples,
posts, horse, burrs--everything dissolves.
Even the moon is edging away.

3.

I know what it is to escape Nebraska.
Right now there are men driving
farther and farther west,
and quickly, in frenzy.
But back here it is night already.
The mercury lights have come on,

34

men are pulling themselves in
from their barns, and now
it begins, if it begins at all,
that active calm of the evening.
In the broad leaves of the cottonwoods,
in farmers' hands, there is
a leftover wind which misses nothing.
Eleazar of Cusa believed it was God.
Funny he did. Who remembers
Eleazar of Cusa? who remembers God?
But in the garden right now,
between leaves, among rows,
in the delicate fabric of moonlight,
there is a presence of absence.
It too has its work,
it too remembers.
Call it the wind of the wind.

(From *The Keeper of Miniature Deer*. Juniper Press. Copyright 1986.
Used with permission of the author.)

KATHLEENE WEST SPEAKS
'HUSKER 'AND ICELANDIC

In an Icelandic city thousands of miles away, a crowd of a hundred people from a dozen countries huddled around a map of America, searching for the pinpoint that was Genoa , Nebraska, and the skinny blue dogleg that was Skeedee Creek.

The woman credited for this international recognition was Kathleene West, who discovered that her poetry spoke a universal language--and received acclaim--in any tongue. She is the first person ever to receive two consecutive Fulbright scholarships to Iceland--a journey which began as a quest to discover her Nebraska roots. In one of her poems, West speaks in the voice of her grandmother coming to Ellis Island and painfully gaining a new identity.

West says the Icelandic experience helped her gain a new feeling of identity as an international poet along with the one she acquired growing up , going to a one-room schoolhouse near Genoa "with eight grades inside and the bathroom outside." "I'm the last of the frontierspeople, I think," said West, who received her Ph.D. degree in English from the University of Nebraska-Lincoln this May.

She discovered "embarrassingly late in life," about 21, that not all poets were long-dead writers who only published in anthologies. Though West decided to become a poet at that age,when someone asked her what she wanted to do with her life, "it was a long time--decades, in fact--before I was arrogant enough to actually say I was a poet."

After eight books and dozens of published poems in journals, magazines and anthologies, West says that "not until fairly recently could I say I was a poet with a straight face."

That doesn't mean, she insists, that she failed to take poetry writing seriously. "I would sit an hour every morning at a desk, scribbling poems with a pen. Like most beginning poets, I thought it was blasphemy to use a typewriter," West said. "Very young poets think typewriting makes writing cold and detached--but that's the reason you should type poems: to get it away from yourself. The typewriter also gives you a sense of what the line looks like, and a line is an integral part of a poem."

The writing began to go someplace when she got a very kind, hand-written rejection slip from Harry Smith of *Smith* magazine, West said. "It would have been so easy for him to make fun of me. Like all beginning poets, my first poems were terrible. But he didn't, so I didn't stop writing." Only later did she discover that beginning writers should start with very small magazines and work upward, West said.

She spent four years as a high school English teacher, then went back to college for a Master's degree, reading every book she could lay her hands on before she published her first book or won the first of many honors.

Achieving international recognition is not the same as becoming a financial success in the world of poetry, West said. "I would love to be corrupted by the influence of money. I think I could live quite nicely." To live as a poet means, for her, teaching at UNL and going on the lecture circuit with her poems.

"It's as hard a life as being a rock star, I think."

Plain Talk from the Platte River

You out there, flanked by mountain ranges,
the foothills dark with soaring fir and cedar,
speak of *plains*
as if you'd lose your breath
scaling the clods turned up by the plow,
as if the creeks had to be kicked
into the rivers, sluggish with boredom under a massive sky
that extends a sameness over miles
and miles of homely soil.

Why should water rush
to get away?
After rain, the Platte's as blue
as Crescent Lake, lingers
as the sun lingers on each glossy leaf
of the willow, the Russian olive,
waits for creeks and the ghosts of creeks
to join its leisurely stretch to the Missouri.
Lost Creek, Disappearing Creek,
Bone, Thin, Dry Creek
name the gullies, the cuts in the earth
where water might settle,
make the latent stream welcome as the child
named before birth.

Birth is a flood, extending generations of seed--
the plains ripple with their growing!
Full-headed wheat, the soft stems of soybeans,
grandly-tassled corn outgrowing its furrow,
and milo, its leaves mimicking the distant flight of birds.
Fields swell with color!

The alfalfa waves crest and break in a spray of purple,
spattering the pastures with mauve.
And always, there is Sunflower
to preside over harvest.
Not corn knife, nor crop duster,
neither nickel-a-dozen bounty nor government spray
will keep away Sunflower.
Constant as the sun,
it nods its bloom across the plains.

This undulant beauty can take away
your breath and fill your eyes with tears.
If you are one to weep for love
or because of love
your tears will hold in the
shallow corners of your eyes
as water seeks its own level
as the river whittles its banks
as the first rain clings to the windowpane
before it drops
and flattens into the earth.

From *Plainswoman: Her First Hundred Years*, 1985 by Sandhills Press, Inc. Used with permission of author.

Kathleene West Photo by Miller and Paine Photographers.

MILDRED BENNETT WROTE UP
A RED CLOUD STORM

Mildred R. Bennett was at the right place at the right time to start the Willa Cather movement in Red Cloud, Nebraska. She and other friends of Cather made Red Cloud one of the most famous villages in American literature.

Thirty years ago, when anyone asked about Willa, most Red Cloud citizens didn't know who was meant. But Bennett changed all that.

It all started when Bennett graduated from Union College in Lincoln and went to Inavale in 1932 to teach in the heart of the farming country of Willa Cather's novels. Many of her pupils were children and grandchildren of the people Willa immortalized in her Nebraska stories.

In November, 1946, Bennett moved to Red Cloud with her doctor husband. Living where Cather grew up gave her access to materials available nowhere else in the world. Her two books on Cather (*The World of Willa Cather* in 1951 and *Early Stories of Willa Cather* in 1957) started the Cather movement and led to a project by the University of Nebraska-Lincoln to collect and publish all of Cather's pre-1912 writings.

In 1955, Bennett and other interested people incorporated the Willa Cather Pioneer Memorial and Educational Foundation, and Bennett has devoted most of her time since then to this memorial. She has served as president, she edits the quarterly Cather newsletter, and she has appeared all over the world talking about Cather. She is recognized as the foremost authority on Willa Cather. This year she wrote a critical paper on *My Mortal Enemy* for inclusion in the 24-page newsletter. She will present that same paper to the Western Literature Association, and her article, "Cather and Religion," will appear in the Brigham Young University magazine.

Bennett was born in Elk Point, South Dakota, and lived many places in the Midwest, because her father was Educational Superintendent for Adventist schools in Iowa, Kansas, Nebraska and South Dakota. She has a B.A. degree from Union College and an M.A. in psychology from UNL.

Recently Bennett finished an autobiographical novel, *The Winters Past*, about a young woman who grew up in a very strict fundamentalist faith and the effects it had on her life.

Bennett has received many honors because of her work on behalf of preserving Cather history. Union College has honored her as an outstanding alumna, and she has received the Henry Fonda Award (1983) and the Nebraska Library Award (1985), among others..

From an unpublished poem:

You may think the brotherhood of man a phrase for
clerics and politicians to mouth
And the atonement happened two thousand years ago.
But don't cut me because when I bleed, you bleed,
 even if you deny the pain.
And the at-one-ment is you and I, and here and now.

From *The World of Willa Cather*

When Willa Cather, daughter of a gentleman sheep-rancher and his patrician Virginia wife, first came to Nebraska in April, 1883, she was a pretty nine-year old with reddish-brown curls, fine skin and dark blue eyes. Her positive personality was apparent even at this age, and friends remember the little girl dressed in a leopard-skin fabric coat and hat sitting on the base shelf in Miner Brothers' General Store in Red Cloud to have a pair of shoes fitted, and discoursing, with some prompting from her father, on Shakespeare, English history, and life in Virginia.

Charles Cather had been toying with the idea of coming West ever since Willa, his first child, was born in 1873. Tuberculosis in the family, the damp climate of Winchester, Virginia, and stories about the new country from earlier homesteaders, including his father and mother and brother George, whetted his interest still more, and when, in 1883, his four-storied sheep barn burned, he and Willa's mother packed up their belongings in Confederate paper currency and took the first train they could get to Red Cloud. The journey, complete with the red-plush seats of the Burlington & Missouri coaches, must have been similar to Willa's description, 35 years later, of young Jim Burden's trip from Virginia to "Black Hawk" (Red Cloud) in the opening pages of the autobiographical *My Antonia.*

Willa's first playmates were the neighbor children, the Lambrechts, whose parents had come from Germany. "Leedy" Lambrecht (the name is now distortedly pronounced Lambert) was the same age as Willa, and played with her in the attic of Grandfather Cather's big frame house. They dressed in adult's garments, pretending to be clowns, or went snake-hunting in the tall grass with Leedy's brother Henry. Henry was bitten by a rattlesnake, and after his parents had given him whiskey (everyone kept it for stomach trouble) and had tied a piece of raw chicken meat over the bite, they took him to Red Cloud where Dr. Damerell put ammonia into the wound. Henry didn't mind the bite so much as he did the day-long bumpy wagon ride, with the road lurching over ridges and through buffalo wallows to enter Red Cloud from the northwest.

From *The World of Willa Cather* , by Mildred Bennett, University of Nebraska Press. Used by permission of the author.

HE TRACKED DOWN STRANGERS OF DUST BOWL DESCENT

Like Luke Skywalker of *Star Wars* fame, Nebraskan Bill Ganzel has been on a travel through time in a search for mysterious strangers he knew only through photographs taken more than 40 years ago -- so that he could take their pictures again.

Remarkably, he found them-- and so did the rest of the world after Ganzel's book, *Of Dust Bowl Descent*, was published in 1984, and the before-and-after photo exhibit which has toured the United States and Europe the past five years is currently on tour in India and the Near East through the U. S. Information Agency.

Ganzel's unusual story began with a chance encounter with a Sheldon Art Gallery exhibit of photographs taken during the Dust Bowl days of the 1930s by the Farm Security Administration. The faces of those Nebraskans haunted Ganzel, who had worked as a newspaper photographer and reporter in small towns before joining the staff of the Nebraska ETV Network.

When the Sheldon director told him there were 80,000 photos taken in the Midwest on file in the National Archives, Ganzel combined a family vacation with an immersion into the voluminous boxes of yellowing prints.

From there, Ganzel wrote a series of grants for money to go through old county records and outdated phone books and call people who had lived in the area where the pictures were taken so many years ago. It was a path down a thousand blind alleys to a few dozen success stories . . . a procedure requiring years of tedious digging, field trips to a hundred farm fields to reshoot the same scenes three decades later.

Through interviews with survivors and their descendants of the Great Depression and Dust Bowl days of the 1930's, Ganzel's story tells the legacy those Nebraskans created for following generations. The book was favorably reviewed by *The New York Times, American Photographer, Christian Science Monitor,* and other newspapers. It won several awards for design. *Life* magazine ran four pages of photographs and text from the book. Ganzel specializes in major documentaries at Nebraska ETV.

His TV programs available to groups include "Riders on the Storm," a documentary on the challenge of water pollution, and "Hand Me Downs," a documentary series of three programs on the folk art of the northern plains. He speaks to groups through a series sponsored by the Nebraska Committee for the Humanities.

From *Of Dust Bowl Descent*

"I been chewing tobacco all my life. I think it preserves the teeth. I never use a toothbrush and I got all my teeth, except one. I could still crack English walnuts with 'em, but my kids told me not to. I used to smoke in them days and I used a bottle cap with small holes in it on the bowl of the pipe. That was for fire prevention, to keep the sparks from jumping out. We had a drought out there. Our chimney--sparks out of it started fires a couple of times, but we got it out.

"I'll put it this way: we just had a plain living. The woman, she'd bake pies once in a while, but that was a luxury. People now live on what I'd say was a luxury them days. The people would get together and they'd have parties, and that didn't cost like it does nowadays. They'd all get together and bring a little to eat, have a little music and dance. Nowadays, to have recreation like we had then, if you hain't got $25 or $30 in your pocket, you better forget about them recreations."

(from *Dust Bowl Descent* by William Ganzel. Used with permission of the author.)

(WILLIAM HURAVITCH Photos. Used with permission of William Ganzel.)

JOHN JANOVY DISCOVERS THE WRITING BUG (AND OTHER EXCITING INSECTS)

John Janovy, Jr. got bitten by the writing bug in the process of exciting discoveries about less exotic insects--like grasshoppers, ticks and fleas.

Keith County Journal, his best-known book, is well on its way to becoming a classic. A screen play based on the book is in the works.

His books are about relationships--the interaction of animals and organisms through the eye of the nature lover, and--in his latest book--the relationship of his basketball-playing daughter to her team. The individual is part of the whole. The group, in this case survives because of the individual--and vice versa.

In the scientific world, Janovy's 34 publications are equally as well-known, dealing with host-parasite relationships and comparative physiology of protozoa. He has been a consultant to the World Health Organization, working with scientists on parasite issues.

The interim director of the University of Nebraska State Museum, professor of life sciences, and director of the Cedar Point Biological Station insists that writing "is an absolute hobby." He writes books because they are, he says, the only appropriate place to make statements about the meaning of his life's work and study. They are both biological and philosophical.

But the scientist/philosopher/professor confesses that "hobby" takes up several hours every day "where I withdraw completely from everybody and everything and write, without fail. To become a scientist is to learn to regularly write large volumes of work," he explains. "I learned lots of skills which help me to organize my beliefs about life into statements which are inescapable to readers."

While *Keith County Journal*, first printed in 1978, is Janovy's statement on the place of parasites and the study of our biological environment, his second book, *Yellowlegs*, 1980, gives his views on scientific research. *Back in Keith County*, 1981, talks about intellectual freedom. *On Becoming a Biologist*, 1985, and *Fields of Friendly Strife*, 1986, relate his experience and philosophy of becoming a scientist and a teacher.

His youngest daughter, Jena (the basketball player--she plays on the University of Nebraska-Omaha team) claims her father is "always the philosopher," as well as a friend and confidante. "He's a typical professor when it comes to answering questions. Ask him what time of day it is, and he will explain the watch."

"Every scientist produces an awful lot of writing," Janovy says. "I approach writing a book with the same feeling I do writing a grant proposal to fund scientific research: when you write for others, you've got to sell yourself first."

The story of his tremendous success makes it sound easy. But Janovy confesses that *Keith County Journal* was rejected 21 times before it found a publisher. *Fields of Friendly Strife* was submitted to 15 publishers before Viking bought it.

The acclaim for his books has outpaced the financial rewards. "It's a lot easier to get famous," Janovy said, "than it is to get rich."

From *Yellowlegs*

You must accept that there are ways of passing vibrations between entities, ways that have yet to be described by any scientist, and not only that, you must accept that I am vulnerable to some of those ways. Those forces jiggle molecules within key cells, and six months ago I could not but feel those forces. I strained to hear the sound again, and again came a *sense* of a call from out in the fog, an insistent call, a wild call, and I remember thinking it was only the cold that sent a shiver of wildness through these forty-year-old bones. I turned first the eyes, then ears, into the mist, straining for the connection, the communication, seeking, needing, asking for the sound that came again and again, and again and again, more strongly then, *the* call, the chorus of calls, the gutteral grating resonant calls, in harmony, in synchrony, over and over, heralding, trumpeting gutteral and resonant, announcing, stronger and stronger and stronger, the wildest sound ever to be heard out on a river, a sound that wrenched the heart in its socket and turned it to the primeval against its will, a sound out of the prehistoric, a sound of total wilderness and insignificance of human being species ill-equipped indeed for life in the *real* wilderness. The sound came rolling through the morning, surrounding, dinning and pounding from every direction, from back into ages when only savages lived, stronger, chorus, gutteral, stronger stronger louder *louder LOUDER* UNTIL AT TREE HEIGHT CAME WAVE UPON WAVE OF GLIDING WINGS SET TO TAKE POSSESSION OF THE AIR AND THE MIND THOUSANDS AND THOUSANDS UPON THOUSANDS OF GRAY ONES ANNOUNCING TO THE WIND THAT THE CRANES HAD RETURNED TO THE RIVER.

They settled into fields, some falling in the most awkward of postures from high out of the mist lifting with the first heat of a sun that had broken through a tree line far to the east. As far as any human could see as the mist moved higher and higher into vapor, there were cranes.

You must know that out on the river with cranes, in the spring upon the Platte in Nebraska, there also returns your feeling that all things are possible. Not only that, there returns the feeling that all things are reasonable, all actions, all ambitions and good ideas, and something has migrated back north with the sandhill cranes. "It's all right to be a biologist after all," you hear yourself saying, "this is my place and these are the things with which I belong." There is a flood and a rush of spring in those thoughts. There is a freedom, a desire, of renewal that can only come back in the spring, rushing into your frozen rituals of the Nebraska Winter in ways that you suddenly realize you've wanted for so many bleak months of darkened cold. I don't know how those feelings and realizations come to the surface in others, but for a biologist, it's sheer orneriness. There was only one thing left to do that day when the cranes returned to the river, and you know without me saying what that one thing was, six months ago.

It doesn't rain much in Nebraska in March, no, most of the rain comes later. But it rains in Kansas in March, and the water accumulates in standing puddles, sometimes several acres in size, off in the corners of some winter wheat field. The sunflowers are dead and brown in March, around those rain puddles, but in March you can see teal out in those puddles, and killdeer along the edges, but most of all you can see real sandpipers. Their long wings cut the prairie air and their legs trail total grace, and they sometimes twist and turn, calling their soft and insistent calls, as they set gliding into that rain puddle off in the corner of some field. And you must know that when you're sitting on that car fender in March, having been called to the river by the wildest sound of all nature, and you know it's rained in Kansas, and it's spring and that flood of freedom and desire for renewal has been released, and that those feelings will come to the surface in a biologist as sheer orneriness, then there's only one thing to do. You punch a cassette into your ancient Mercury's tape player, with Bill Monroe and the wildest call of the five string banjo, turn it up full blast volume, and aim that second-hand piece of junk out hurtling across the prairies south into Kansas to see if you can find a yellowlegs.

(From *Yellowlegs*. St. Martin's Press, Inc. Copyright 1980. Used with permission of the author.)

PAUL JOHNSGARD'S WORLD HAS BIRDS, UNICORNS AND A 'SHAGGY DRAGON'

A huge white swan swoops, suspended, above his head as Paul Johnsgard leans over the computer keys in his office, pounding out a half-dozen major books a year.

The life-size bird was painstakingly carved in the spring of 1984 while the University of Nebraska-Lincoln Foundation Professor of Biological Sciences was home recuperating from a heart attack. As the graceful swan's wings grew under his skilled knife, Johnsgard said he felt ready to fly at his usual pace, too--a creative output that makes him the most prolific of all living ornithological writers and one of the most frequently honored professors in the history of the University of Nebraska.

Author of 19 published books, the internationally-recognized scientist has received the Wildlife Society's highest honor for publications. He is one of only two persons in UNL's history to receive all three of the University's major faculty awards. In 1984 he won the Mari Sandoz Award for his writing.

His interest in birds started when an aunt gave him a copy of Audubon's famous bird directory for his eighth birthday. "I was living out on the edge of things in a little town in North Dakota," Johnsgard recalls. "I literally memorized that book. My goal in life was someday to become a waterfowl census taker like my uncle."

Bird-watching has remained the love --and the art--of his life.

A college classroom assignment to categorize Midwest waterfowl led Johnsgard to decide to catalog all North American species and publish his first book before he graduated from college. But another 25 years passed before Johnsgard wrote his first popular book.

"I put off writing my book about the snow goose for years, afraid of what my colleagues would say. Now I've learned I can afford to take those kinds of chances, and writing the popular books is one of the most delightful experiences for me."

47

Johnsgard illustrates most of his own books. One of his latest books, *Dragons and Unicorns,* was co-written by his daughter, Karin, a student at Nebraska Wesleyan University.

Prairie Children, Mountain Visions shows the value of "worthless animals," such as one he calls a "stegosaurus." Johnsgard refers to it, with a twinkle in his eye, as his "shaggy dragon story. All you have to believe," he said, "is that the species didn't become extinct when everybody else thought it did."

The young readers' books were created because, Johnsgard said, "that's the age we have to reach with messages about how to save our ecology, birds, plants and the rest. By the teen years, they may be too set in their values. I think kids are growing up without much sense of what their environment is worth," he said.

"Reaching children is at least as important as reaching scientists."

From *Those of the Gray Wind*

PREFACE

For nearly six months the rivers and shallow marshes of eastern North Dakota are locked in the merciless grip of winter. By late March the snow begins to melt and flows into creeks and ditches that make their way to the Red River of the North. This river, which empties into Lake Winnipeg, drains the table-flat valley that once was the bottom of glacial Lake Agassiz. The Red River technically originates at an old Indian camping site once called Chahinkapa ("Opening in the Trees") and later named Wahpeton ("Dwellers Among the Leaves"). From this point, at the confluence of the Ottertail River, which has its origin in the glacial moraine of western Minnesota, and the Bois de Sioux, whose source is the northern overflow channel of Lake Traverse, the Red River flows north.

Lake Traverse, located just south of the point where the two Dakotas meet Minnesota, is the southernmost point on the drainage that collects the water flowing northward through the Red River Valley, finally reaching Hudson Bay. A few miles farther south is Big Stone Lake, the outlet of which flows into the Minnesota River, then into the Mississippi, and finally south into the Gulf of Mexico. Separating the lakes is a narrow valley floor that forms a drainage divide, the significance of which is overlooked by nearly everyone who travels the adjacent highways. Yet, the Traverse-Big Stone region marks not only a continental watershed boundary but also is the last area of extensive marshland south of the heavily cultivated Red River Valley. Furthermore, it is the halfway point on the 2,500-mile migration route of the snow geese between their Gulf Coast wintering grounds and their Hudson Bay nesting areas.

Lake Traverse represents a natural magnet for migrating water birds, which gain some protection from winter winds by the adjacent hills and find abundant food in the lake's shallows or in the nearby agricultural uplands. To this rendezvous each spring come hordes of canvasbacks and whistling swans, which after leaving their wintering grounds in Chesapeake Bay follow the valley of the Minnesota River northwestward across southern Minnesota. From the Gulf of Mexico come redheads, ruddy ducks, and lesser scaups; from the rivers and marshes of the Southern States and Mexico come green-winged teal, gadwalls, and common mergansers. For a few memorable weeks each year, between the end of March and the last week of April, these ducks and swans share Lake Traverse with one another and with the wild geese, forming a pantheon of waterfowl. Wild Canada geese are there, ranging from four-pound birds on their way to Baffin Island nesting grounds to ten- or twelve-pound "honkers" that will breed only a few hundred miles farther north. The watchful eye can also see white-fronted geese, which remain aloof from all the others and keep warily to the remotest parts of the lake. But the jewels of the lake are the snow geese.

By the first week of April the vanguards of the snow geese have arrived. Riding a south wind and a cloudless sky, they leave the broad valleys of the Missouri River not far from Sioux City. Under starry skies they fly northward, passing above the sacred red pipestone quarries of southwestern Minnesota, reaching Big Stone and Traverse lakes by dawn. Then, on tired wings, they snowflake downward into the waiting marsh at the north end of Lake Traverse.

As a boy growing up in Wahpeton, I measured my winters, not in terms of conventional time intervals, but in the days until the geese returned to Lake Traverse. By late March I could find scattered groups of mallards and pintails in thawing creeks near town, but it wasn't until the first haunting cries of the wild geese penetrated the evening air that schoolwork became drudgery and the only important event of the day was the weekend weather forecast. When Saturday finally came, the family car would be loaded with a change of clothes, a thermos or two, hip boots, binoculars and, when I had finally saved enough money to buy them, a camera and telephoto lens. Within half an hour I would be simultaneously jockeying the car through the muddy and badly rutted country roads of northern South Dakota and searching the horizon for flying geese. By midmorning the birds were heading back into the marsh after their morning foraging session in adjacent fields, and it was only a short time before the direction of their movements made apparent the best location to hide in order to intercept their flightlines.

This annual spring ritual of meeting the geese on their return from the south was more important to me than the opening day of the hunting season, the beginning of summer vacation, or even the arrival of Christmas. The spring return of the geese represented my epiphany, a manifestation of gods I could see, hear, and nearly touch as the streamed into the marsh a few feet above the tips of the cattails and phragmites. By evening I would be wet, cold, and exhausted from wading through icy waters and crawling through mud and snow. But during the drive home my ears would resound with the cries of the wild geese and, when I closed my eyes that night, I saw them still, their strong wings flashing in the sunlight, their immaculate bodies projected against the azure sky. They were my criterion of beauty, my definition of wildness, my vision of paradise. I had little idea of where they had come from and even less conception of where they were headed. I knew only that I must be there to see them, to become a vicarious part of something I couldn't begin to understand, but which to me represented the primordial energy of life.

(From *Those of the Gray Wind.* Copyright 1981 by Paul Johnsgard, St. Martin's Press, New York. Used with permission of the author.)

Johnsgard photo by George Tuck.

ROBERT MANLEY MAKES HISTORY
A PERSONAL STORY

A fourth grade boy in northeastern Nebraska recently told Robert Manley what he had learned from his history book: "I am my grandfather's future."

"He summed up the whole thing. I couldn't have said it better myself," Dr. Manley admitted. He became a writer, he said," to teach that special view of history to children and adults who never learned that it's about me and my world--not somebody else."

He shares the views in his 12 books, on a series of published cassette tapes about Nebraska history, and has done a Nebraska ETV series, "Rails West," which received the Ohio State University award for social studies.

Manley was named the Outstanding High School Teacher in Nebraska, and, later, the Student's Professor at the University of Nebraska-Lincoln. At UNL he wrote his first book as an assignment for the history department. *Frontier University*, published by the University of Nebraska Press, was immediately successful--and Manley found an urge to write he never had before.

However, a fellow academic warned Manley he had no future: "The problem is that people can understand everything you write."

A public historian for 20 years, Manley could care less whether some professor characterizes him as a popularizer. "I have an audience that needs what I have to offer," he said.

What makes him enthusiastic about writing is the audience, says Manley, who speaks to thousands of school children every year. "It's exciting to show them through history that there's a future--a time ahead."

The author says his book called *The Minden Farmers Co-Op: The First 75 Years*, which has now sold more than 12,000 copies, is one of his most important works. "The co-op movement in Nebraska is one of the most significant things that's happened to agriculture. It affects all small towns in the state. "This kind of book lets people know that there's history in their own hometown." *The Meaning of Brownville*, published by the Nebraska Committee for the Humanities, serves the same purpose, he said.

Most schools Manley visits tell him history is the school's weakest subject, the author/historian said. "That's because history hasn't been localized by the academic community for teachers who go out into the school systems.

Children share his view of academics as dull or dead, Manley said. "When I go into a school where the students have watched me on TV and the filmstrips, they greet me as a star," he said. "When I meet children who have only read my textbooks, they look at me and never know just what to say."

From *Nebraska--Our Pioneer Heritage*

In the 1870s a Nebraska newspaper editor wrote, "Nebraska has caught a bad case of railroad fever!"

He was right. Every Nebraska town-builder wanted a railroad built to his town. All over Nebraska people were talking about railroads. Railroads would bring prosperity to Nebraska.

The railroad companies often asked towns and counties for money. After all, said the railroad companies, it cost a great deal of money to build railroads. The towns and counties should help pay for building the railroads.

So the people in the towns and counties voted bonds for the railroads. The money from the bonds was given to the railroads. The people then paid taxes for many years in order to pay off the bonds.

The railroad meant life or death for a prairie town. What happened to towns that did not get a railroad? Many towns died. Others like Brownville practically disappeared.

Brownville's citizens had voted thousands of dollars in bonds to build a railroad. But the men who ran the railroad company were crooks. They took Brownville's money but never built the railroad. The people who lived in Brownville had to pay for the bonds they had given to the company. Taxes became very, very high; and people moved away from Brownville. Because of the railroad that was never built, the town of Brownville almost died.

Some town-builders just moved their stores and houses across the prairie to a new town site along the railroad. The railroads wanted to have stations or depots every eight or ten miles along their tracks. This made it easy for farmers, who used horse-drawn wagons, to bring their crops to the stations. And, of course, usually a little town grew up around the station or depot.

What was it like to ride on a pioneer railroad train?

Traveling on these first trains was exciting, but not very comfortable. The passengers sat on hard wooden benches. On hot summer days the windows were wide open. Smoke, soot and sparks poured in upon the passengers.

At night, flickering candles or a few kerosene lanterns provided a little light. During the winter the people in the cars were always cold. A small coal-burning stove at one end of the car could not keep the people warm.

Eating was a problem. Many people carried food with them. Other passengers jumped from the cars when the train stopped at a depot. Most depots had an "eating house" where passengers could buy a meal. Usually the train stopped for twenty or thirty minutes so the passengers could eat.

Since the tracks were rough, the cars bounced and swayed from side to side. Although the trains went slowly--fifteen or twenty miles an hour was the top speed for passenger trains--the passengers in the car were frequently bounced from their seats.

JAMES McKEE DESCRIBES LINCOLN 'LOVE AFFAIR'

Jim McKee has had a lifelong love affair with Lincoln. Not only has this given him ample opportunity to write about Lincoln, but it has also led him to serve on more than 17 art and business boards in his home town.

McKee is a native Lincolnite. In fact, his grandparents--all four of them--pioneered in Lancaster County. So his knowledge and history of Lincoln/Lancaster County span three generations of firsthand information.

He is a prime example of "write what you know"--he's authored more than 350 articles and books on Nebraska and related history. His *Lincoln, the Prairie Capital* is a popular coffee table picture history book.

McKee has taken his historical pursuit one step further: He has developed the "Lincoln Trivia Game."

He is also the official historian for the City of Lincoln.

McKee edits "The Nebraska NEWSLETTER," teaches a local history class at Southeast Community College, serves as a consultant to the Lincoln Public School System, and has a seasonal radio show on KLIN, "That's the Way It Was."

When asked how he got the information for his books, articles and talks, he said, "It's just like Topsy--it just grew. I studied things that interested me, and I became an antique collector: I collected photographs and books and originally had as much interest in that as I did in the history itself."

He recently participated in an all-day workshop on story telling and writing. He talked to writers about self-publishing. He says, "It's just one other way to get your work published." His books, only one of which is still in print, are not self-published.

McKee gives 20 different slide and storytelling programs on local and state history. "The most popular one," he states, "depicts the early history of Lincoln and Lancaster County from their origins." His programs vary in length from 30 minutes to two hours.

His love of books and good literature led McKee to open a bookstore, Lee Booksellers, in Lincoln. He is also interested in coins. But mainly, McKee is interested in Lincoln.

From *Lincoln: The Prairie Capital*

One of Lincoln's best-known citizens, William Jennings Bryan, was born in 1860 in Salem, Illinois, where his father practiced law and was later made a judge. About the only distinguishing feature of his childhood and university days was that he was orator for his graduating class in both high school and master's law class. He began practicing law in 1883 and on one occasion visited a classmate, A.R. Talbot, in Lincoln. He was so impressed with the city that he determined to move to the prairie capital.

On his arrival in 1887 he established his practice in the Burr Block at 12th and O and, surviving on a scant income, lived for a few months in the office, sleeping on a couch and cooking over a gas ring. It was at this point that he became interested in the Democratic party and began making speeches on its behalf. In 1890 Bryan was elected to the U.S. Congress, where he served two terms. From 1894 to 1896, he was editor of the Omaha *World-Herald*. At the Democratic National Convention in 1896 his keynote address, the still-famous "Cross of Gold" speech, so stirred the delegates that he found himself nominated for the Presidency.

Using his famed powers of oratory, Bryan campaigned more vigor - ously than virtually any predecessor. It was his idea that by talking directly to the voters, he could convince them of the validity of his candidacy. The result was the nation's first "whistle-stop campaign." He traveled more than 20,000 miles and talked to hundreds of thousands of people, but was defeated nonetheless. He was nominated again in 1900, and that same year he founded his own newspaper, *The Commoner*, in Lincoln. Bryan felt that his home on D street was not suitable for a potential United States President and began planning "Fairview" at 49th and Sumner, which he envisioned as a "Monticello of the west." He lost in 1900, and again in 1908, but in his campaigns had become well known as an orator and was much sought after on the Chautauqua circuits. He was named Secretary of State by Woodrow Wilson in 1913 and received a great deal of national publicity in 1915 when he resigned in protest over actions that Bryan felt could draw the United States into war with Germany. Bryan died in 1925, a few days after the highly publicized and controversial Scopes evolution trial, in which he was opposed by Clarence Darrow. At his death Bryan was said to be the highest-priced public speaker in the world, commanding a minimum of $1,000 per appearance. He was said to have spoken directly to more people than any other person in history, a record still standing today because of the modern reliance on radio and television.

SHE FOUND HERSELF IN
A LOST LADY

Who would suspect that reading a book for fun could change your life? But that's exactly what happened when five years ago Sue Rosowski read Willa Cather's book, A Lost Lady and found her new life's work.

The book started out as a kind of self-reward, kind of like enjoying chocolate chip cookies and ice cream, after a hard day's work on a "serious" topic: her doctoral dissertation in eighteenth-century literature.

"Things like this just happen when you least expect it," admits Rosowski, who now is regarded as the nation's preeminent Cather scholar and author.

"I kept giving myself more Cather as a reward. I'd tell myself that if I wrote five pages on the dissertation, I could read more Cather," she confessed. "Then, almost before I realized what was happening, Cather had moved to the center of my thoughts."

Rosowski's writing career began by writing about Cather. "And once that happened, I became really hooked. Each book is a new world that leads to three others."

"I found myself very excited by reading--and by the sense that books have lives of their own which we live into for a while."

"A while" for Rosowski is several hours a day, which she takes in seclusion in a tiny room behind locked doors on the fourth floor of Love Library doing what she loves best--"bringing order out of words."

When we're in a time that seems so much out of control, it seems so healthy to use reading and writing to bring a sense of order," says the professor of English teaching Cather studies and writing at the University of Nebraska-Lincoln.

"I'll be reading along and, all of a sudden, get an 'Aha! So that's how I can explain The Song of the Lark . So that's what lies at the heart of Sapphira and the Slave Girl." Beginning in 1986, Rosowski will produce the first scholarly edition of Cather's works under a major grant by the Woods Foundation in an effort to describe how all the pieces of Cather's works fit together as a canon.

"Nothing is more exciting than discovering words," she said, "and through them coming to see your world more clearly and communicating with others in an extremely powerful way."

"Just try it out. Write for yourself--just because it's a pleasure for you."

"I can't imagine life without writing," confesses this author, wife, professor, critical researcher, and mother of two children. "It's what keeps everything else in my world in balance."

From *The Voyage Perilous*

Cather's early essays and stories lay out the terms of her lifelong commitment to vindicating imaginative thought in a world grown material. Her novels, the major subjects of this study, develop that commitment. The initial novels explore the nature of the imagination and celebrate its power; the middle works offer the imagination as a vehicle by which the individual might wrest personal salvation from an increasingly alien world; the late novels are Gothic tales in which the imagination breaks through not to "divine truths" but to darkness.

In her early writing Cather explored the terms of imaginative thought and celebrated creativity. Her first novel, *Alexander's Bridge* (1912), is an allegory about the romantic imagination in its most primitive form, energy flowing between the spiritual world and the physical one. Cather aptly viewed *Alexander's Bridge* as an apprentice work in which she laid out the materials she would later employ; it is a book about the romantic imagination more than an example of it. As such, it prepared the way for *O Pioneers!* (1913), a two-part pastoral charged with the energy of an artist revelling in her now-found imaginative power to create beauty from both triumph and tragedy. In the first part, Cather drew upon Virgilian pastoral tradition to celebrate a communal myth of New World paradise; in the second, she drew upon a modern pastoral tradition to exalt a private paradise within an alien world. With its yoking of classical and romantic materials, *O Pioneers!* serves as a paradigm for Cather's most successful writing, in which she infused a romantic mode with classical myths.

In her next novel Cather again wrote of the imagination, this time in more personal terms. *The Song of the Lark* (1915) is Willa Cather's *Prelude*, in which she used an autobiographical character to trace the growth of an artist's mind. In doing so Cather explored a theme that runs through modern literature, the development of a personal self to serve as a source of value in an otherwise common world, private and public.

These are the terms that Cather incorporated into the narrative structure of *My Antonia* (1918), in which a subject (Jim Burden) writes of an "object" (Antonia). Here Cather for the first time wrote a fully developed literature of process. The novel is about the capacity of the mind to perceive symbols as self-generating sources of meaning. The narrator, Jim Burden, states a differentia of modern literature inherited from the Romantics when he writes that Antonia "had always been one to leave images in the mind that did not fade--that grew stronger with time."

In *One of Ours* (1922) Cather wrote of the tragedy of a man who lacks this symbol-making capacity. Here Cather retained the romantic terms of subject and object, but instead of celebrating the reconciliation of the two, she stressed the disparity between them. This book in which Cather explored a character's failure of the imagination preceded that in which she most fully realized its creative potential. *A Lost Lady* (1923) is a carefully modulated romantic prose-poem. In it, as in a Keatsian ode, subject and object engage in dialectic movement, with moments of wholeness followed by separation, of illusion followed by disappointment.

Following *A Lost Lady* Cather asked a question that had run as an undercurrent through her previous writing: what is left when the imagination fades and the world is fallen? In *The Professor's House* (1925) Cather told a romantic version of the Fall by introducing St. Peter as one who has suffered a lapse in perception, from creative imagination to reason, then setting him on a quest for redemption. By casting off ties to the outside world, St. Peter liberates from within himself dreams that contain archetypal truths. In doing so, he reaches an essential unity of symbolic forms. Then, as if preparing for the new key in which she would write, Cather in *My Mortal Enemy* (1926) created characters who reject a romanticism that had deteriorated into sentimentality.

After *My Mortal Enemy*, Cather turned away from the old dichotomy. By creating characters who had denied their personal selves and putting them in the most alien of settings, she revised her literary problem, no longer asking how subject and object meet and instead presenting a unity antecedent to dualism. In *Death Comes to the Archbishop* (1927) two Catholic priests disciplined to erase their individual selves make their way through a desert; in *Shadows on the Rock* (1931) a slight apothecary and his young daughter lead lives of quiet renunciation on a rock suspended in a Canadian wilderness. Using these most unlikely of materials, Cather celebrated the Harmony of correspondences. No longer concerned with using language to mediate between self and other, she embraced possibilities recognized by the symbolist, who "redefines the whole process of knowing," then deliberately experiments "with alogical structures of multiple meanings."

Finally, *Lucy Gayheart* (1935) and *Sapphira and the Slave Girl* (1940) are Gothic novels in which Cather explored the underside of the romantic imagination. In these, her last books, Cather confronted head-on the threat that runs through her writing, as through romanticism in general: that the imagination will break through not to ultimate truths but to evil, chaos, and--worst of all--nothingness.

(From *The Voyage Perilous*. Copyright 1986 by the University of Nebraska Press. Used with permission.)

A REAL-LIFE COWBOY SPURRED NELLIE YOST INTO WILD-WEST WRITING

His name was Pinnacle Jake, a real cowboy in Wyoming and Montana, and people were spellbound by his stories.

When his daughter, Nellie Snyder Yost, feared the tales would die out with her dad, "I simply let him tell them to me in his own words." By the time he got through, she had her first book.

But selling it was some-thing else. "I was past 40 years old and hadn't ever done any writing," recalls the author who has just won another Silver Spur award for the Best Story of the Year by the Western Writers of America--40 years later.

WWA also presented her with the Golden Saddleman in 1975, the highest award given for "bringing dignity and honor to the history and legends of the west." And Yost won the Wrangler trophy by the Cowboy Hall of Fame in Oklahoma City for *Buffalo Bill*, the best non-fiction book published in 1979. David Hartman interviewed her on "Good Morning America."

She has received dozens of honors for her writing and historical research, and is the only woman ever chosen to be Grand Marshal of an Old Glory Blowout and a colonel in the Cody Scouts of North Platte.

During the early years, writing was a luxury there was little time to indulge. Born in a sod house, she was valedictorian of Maxwell High School 60 years ago. She taught in a one-room schoolhouse, riding horseback six miles a day to school. Her early years of marriage and motherhood were spent on a Sandhills ranch, with no thought of writing.

At first, she said, she wondered if she would ever get published.

Pinnacle Jake was rejected by several publishers. "It makes you wonder yourself whether you're any good as a writer," she admits. "But I'll never forget that first acceptance. That was a great day!"

Then came an invitation to join the Nebraska Writers Guild. Mari Sandoz, the Story-Catcher of the Plains, was to be the featured speaker at a Guild meeting. "I wrote to her, but I was so in awe of her," Yost recalls. "I was amazed she was so friendly. She urged me to go ahead, and I felt for the first time like I had a little guidance and direction."

With that spur, Yost says, "I got right busy. In six weeks I'd written *The West That Was* with John Leaky, then my mother's story, *No Time on My Hands*, which has just been reprinted by the University of Nebraska Press."

She still does the first draft of her stories in longhand "so I can erase," and writes each one three times to polish.

"Every day I write, beginning early in the morning. I used to write all day and into the evenings," she said. But experience and success and time have taken their toll on her energy. These days she stops writing at noon, using afternoons and evenings for public speaking and continuing board work for the State Historical Society, on which she has served for more than 20 years.

At 80+ Yost, a recent bride of poet Frank Lydic, says she can report the same thing of herself as she wrote about her mother: She's yet to find a day with time on her hands.

From *No Time on My Hands*

That afternoon Mama sent Florry and me to the melon patch to get a good melon for supper. It would freeze any night now and spoil all that were left in the patch, she said.

Poppie had raised a fine crop of beans and melons on the new sod field across the canyon, and for weeks we had hauled the big, sweet melons home by the wagonload. The vines in the patch were withered and stringy now, and the melons small, but in a corner of the patch, under a whopping big tumbleweed, we found the biggest melon of them all. Waist high to the two of us, perfectly round and smooth, it had grown unseen all summer. We had carried other melons home by gathering them up in our aprons and toting them across the canyon on our stomachs, but this one was far too big for that. So we rolled it home. Across the field and down the near side of the deep canyon, across the bottom and up the far slope to the house. Several times we almost let it slip from our sweaty hands, and near the end of the trip we hardly had breath or strength to push it any farther, but at last we brought it safe to the kitchen door.

In all my life I have never eaten a sweeter, better melon.

Two or three days of damp, cloudy weather followed our trip to the melon patch, and when the sky cleared at sundown Poppie said we'd sure get a killing frost that night, it was so clear and still.

The next afternoon, after the heavy frost had melted, Poppie took Florry and me to the bean patch and showed us how to pull and rick the dead vines. Before he left he warned us not to eat any of the melons left in the field beside the beans. They'd make us sick, now that they'd been frosted, he said.

Florry and I, working alone in the beans through the sunny October days, had a hot, tiresome, dirty job on our hands. One afternoon when we had finished off the water in our bottle, we got so thirsty we went into the melon patch, broke open some of the best-looking melons and ate the hearts. They tasted slick, and too sweet, and we felt bad about disobeying Poppie, but we ate enough to kill our thirst and then back to bean pulling.

"You girls've been eating those frosted melons, haven't you?" Moma said as soon as we came in the door that evening. We looked at each other, wondering how in the world she knew.

"I can tell because your faces are cleaner around your mouths than anywhere else," she said, "and I just hope you aren't sick tonight."

But we were--cramping and throwing up most of the night, and unable to go back to the field until the next afternoon. When we left, Mama said she guessed we'd know better than to eat any more of the melons.

We pulled the last of the beans a few days later and then, because there was still quite a piece of the afternoon left, we stayed to play awhile in the melon patch--and so we found another mammoth melon. Late grown on the end of a vine that had wandered clear out of the patch, it had been protected from the frost by the heavy growth of grass and weeds that had hidden it so long and it looked fresh and crisp. We decided to break it open and try it. If it tasted slick, like those that had made us sick, we wouldn't eat it. But it tasted every bit as good as the earlier melons, so we ate all we could hold of it and threw the rest in the weeds where Poppie wouldn't see it when he came to haul the beans home.

Then we looked at each other. Sure enough, besides a guilty look, we each had a too-clean patch around our mouths. We fixed that by rubbing some dust into the sticky juice on our faces, and then went on home. But we must have overdone it a little; for as soon as Mama saw us she said, "You girls've been eating those melons again. Just wait till Poppie finds out."

We didn't get sick that time, but we got spanked for not minding.

(From *No Time on My Hands*. Copyright by Nellie Snyder Yost. Reprinted by the University of Nebraska Press, 1986. Used with permission of the author.)

A FUNNY THING HAPPENED TO TERESA BLOOMINGDALE

Teresa Bloomingdale of Omaha is probably Nebraska's most successful humor wirter--five books in six years for a contract well into six figures.

She has two agents: a writer's agent and a speaker's agent.

Bloomingdale gives a talk to women's groups called "A Funny Thing Happened on the Way to My Career." The "funny thing" she talks about is that, upon graduation from college in Omaha, she married a young lawyer (a Creighton Uni - versity graduate) and they had ten children in the next 12 years.

So her career got put on "hold."

Bloomingdale grew up in St. Joseph, Missouri, where her father was editor of *The News-Press.* Her father's being a journalist was not the deciding factor in her becoming a writer, though. That decision was not made until the '60s, when she was already a mother and homemaker.

"Women were beginning to do things in the '60s (besides staying home and having families). I tried to think of what I could do. The only thing I knew about was having 10 children. So I began writing about having 10 children."

Her "off the wall" humor in a monthly column in a national Catholic magazine caught the attention of Doubleday & Company in 1978. They negotiated a contract with her to do five books in the next six years.

If she wasn't busy writing before, she was then! "I never really intended to write books," she said. "I was snookered into it by Doubleday."

All five of her books are being translated into German, and all but one are in paperback.

Because of her wonderful sense of the comic, she was approached by a feminist greeting card company to do some "one liners" for a series of cards. She sent fifty--they used three. A year later she received a huge check.

She was also a contributing editor to *McCall's* and a regular on Vicki Lawrence's morning show on USA Network.

She says ,"You have to be prepared to do a lot of things (to promote a book)." She went to a lot of booksellers' conventions, did a lot of radio and television shows, appeared with a lot of celebrities ("People like a celebrity connection").

Five years ago a major New York speakers bureau contacted her to appear on its lecture circuit. She was already doing a lot of appearances, so she was glad to turn the business of bookings and travel arrangements over to them. She travels thousands of miles each month to fulfill speaking obligations.

Bloomingdale's office is spotlessly clean. She has a computer, so instead of the piles and piles of paper that usually accompany writing, she has a little box of floppy disks.

She just sent the manuscript of a mystery book to her agent, and she is currently working on a sequel. She hopes there will be a series. "Mysteries go fast," she said. "It took me about three months to finish the first one." She says it's like the British murder mysteries: "Three die, but you don't see any heads rolling, no blood gushing."

One word of advice Bloomingdale gives writers is "Don't nag your agent (or editor, or publisher). You might like to, but don't."

Teresa Tries Her Hand on Wall Street

Okay, Muffy, I admit it. I am a principal passenger on the Buckley bandwagon, which has been chugging along steadily for some years now, but has picked up steam since big brother Jim agreed to put down his birdwatching binoculars and save the country.

My fellow columnist Muffy Fisher, thinks I have a THING about William F. Buckley, Jr. and, though she understands it, (being a former fan of WFB,) she wants me to switch my allegiance to Louis Rukeyser, moderator of Wall Street Week, another of the increasingly popular Educational Television shows.

Muffy's right, of course. I do have a thing about Bill Buckley. He is brash, bold, often inaccurate, sometimes impolite, and a real snob. But I love his wit, his way with words, his brilliance and his beliefs, and most of all I love his mother. Mrs. Buckley is a true lady; she is charming, gracious, witty and wise, and besides that she has managed to keep her sanity while raising ten raucous, rambunctious, super-active children, which naturally makes her my ideal.

I also love Bill's sister, Aloise, herself the mother of ten children, who found time, amid diapers and dishes, housework and homework, to write hilarious essays about her children. (See her book *Will Mrs. Majors Go to Hell?* Arbor House) Which naturally makes her my ideal, too.

But if there's anything I am good at, it's taking advice, so I took Muffy's and watched Mr. Rukeyser's show. It was my Waterloo. The fellow convinced me that even a dum-dum like me can make a killing in the stock market, so I embezzled from my grocery budget and bought five shares of a respectable, conservative stock. That was at 2:00 Tuesday.

At 4:00 I hastily and nervously checked the evening paper to see how my stock was doing. Down 1/8. A depression! Now I knew how Grandpa felt in '29! I couldn't eat dinner. I spent the evening fiddling with the radio trying to get late stock market news. (Have you ever spent four hours listening to AM radio? My God, the music!)

I couldn't sleep. I lay awake all night wondering how the Rockefellers ever managed to get any rest. At 5:00 the morning paper hit the porch. I bounded out of bed, dashed to the door, tore open the paper, only to discover my stock was still down 1/8. Those idiots hadn't even worked last night. The country was headed for financial disaster and nobody cared. Wouldn't you think the Exchange would stay open all night just to see if, per chance, my stock would go up?

At 8:00 A.M. I called my broker. He wasn't in yet. No wonder the stock market is in such bad shape. Two hours later he returned my call.

"Sell!" I demanded hysterically.

"But you just bought it," he argued. "Anyway, the stock is already back up. And if you sell now, you'll lose the commission."

"I don't care," I said. "It's worth it to get rid of the worry." So I sold, and a week later the stock was up 10 points. I hope the Rockefellers realize how I've added to their riches.

Sorry, Muffy, I'm going back to Buckley. Mr. Rukeyser lures my money, of which I have very little, while Mr. Buckley will settle for my laughs.

And I've got a lot of unused laughs lying around.

From *Sense and Momsense*

If you want to please your mother, talk to her. If you want to make points with your father, listen to him.

Teresa Bloomingdale photo by Marvin Reese Photographers.

CUNNINGHAM'S STORIES AS BIG AS A NEBRASKA BACKYARD

Reba Pierce Cunningham of Lincoln is a dimunitive woman, and her size might mislead you into thinking her writing style is just as dainty. On the contrary, her stories are as big as all outdoors—which is where they take place.

This tiny woman was a beauty queen at Valparaiso University in Indiana. She transferred to Iowa State University, where she met and married John Sloss, a popular young football player who was interested in ranching. After graduation, they moved to Ft. Robinson. From there, they took their two-year-old son and moved to a ranch in Montana. They ranched there and in Wyoming until John's death. Cunningham continued ranching for a time after husband's death, then moved to Nebraska to be near her son, who is now a pathologist.

Cunningham's stories are about those years on the ranch. She has just written a book, *Cowboys, Cooks and Catastrophes,* about one facet of life on the ranch. These stories are about the many cooks who came and went—bunkhouse cooks, all characters—whom Cunningham was in charge of hiring, firing, training, cajoling, and "You name it, I did it."

Cunningham began her writing career in 1960 with an article she sold to *Guideposts* magazine. From that beginning she went on to write regularly for *The Denver Post* (for five years). *The San Francisco Chronicle, the Great Falls Tribune, Western Horseman,* and *The Omaha World-Herald* also bought her stories.

When the manuscript of *Cowboys, Cooks, and Catastrophes* was finished two years ago, a friend took the book to a meeting of Western Writers of America (Cunningham is a member) and gave it to the editor of *True West* and *Frontier Times.* He bought nine of the stories to run as a serial in those magazines. After that, Barbed Wire Press bought the book—which contains a dozen stories of hilarious episodes with cowboys, cooks and catastrophes—and published it in time for Christmas season in 1985. It is a fun, funny book.

Since then, Cunningham has completed a book-length manuscript using third and fourth grade children's writings, which she calls *How Do You Do It? Ask a Kid.* She is also collaborating with an Arizona writer on a novel based on a true story about a Montana madam. Meantime, she continues to to sell articles to newspapers and magazines. She writes her first drafts in pen, then edits and rewrites in final form on a typewriter.

Cunningham is also working on another book, not quite so humorous, which tells stories she thinks should be saved because they tell about the Old West.

She does not keep the money from the sale of her books and articles. She sends it to foundations that feed starving children everywhere.

From *Cowboys, Cooks, and Catastrophes.* Copyright 1985. Artwork used with permission of Bud McCaulley and Barbed Wire Press.

From *Cowboys, Cooks and Catastrophes*

Pat and His False Teeth

After several bouts suffering with ulcerated teeth, I insisted on old Pat having the old snags pulled. I felt duty bound to help him break in his new dentures. During this time, his cussing was more poignant than ever. He would run me down several times a day, remove the bits of crockery from under his gray beard, with portions of his last meal still clinging to them, thrust them under my nose and point out each offending tooth. "Now, ma'am, see this one? It rubs my gums back and forth, back and forth, until they're sore as hell. That tooth sure's got it in for me. And see this one? It hangs on to everythin' I just et and won't let go. And this one jus goes up and down, up and down, and won't stop. Now, these two in the front bite like a bulldog. Don't my tongue look like its been bit to you?" He stuck it out for me to see.

Pat's teeth fit so loosely he was always losing them and you could expect them to turn up in the most unusual places. We could always track them down. But there was the day they could not be found. Pat had us all looking for them. We looked along the irrigation ditch that ran through the garden, under the vegetables, in the milking stall and chicken house. No teeth! We decided thay would never be found and Pat's eating juicy, red apples and buttered popcorn days were over.

That afternoon, as Etta dumped out a bushel basket of green string beans to snap for supper, along with them came Pat's false teeth, as big as life.

(From *Cowboys, Cooks, and Catastrophes*. Copyright by Reba Pierce Cunningham, 1985, Barbed Wire Press. Used with permission of the author.)

DUANE HUTCHINSON TELLS TALES IN AND OUT OF SCHOOL

"Tell me a story."

To answer this basic human need in a way that can set people's hair on end or make them laugh or cry is a true art form, according to Duane Hutchinson, who makes his living telling--and writing--tall tales.

His favorite genre is ghost stories, which is a common thread for every age group, says Hutchinson, who has given more than 5,000 programs in the last seven years. He especially likes "The Ghost of Nebraska Wesleyan," the tale of a music teacher at the university who died in the school in the early part of the century with recurrent reports of sightings of her image in campus buildings since then.

Hutchinson came by the skill the way most of us do, he confesses-- hearing stories just too good to keep to himself. As a boy he remembers neighboring Sandhills ranchers would gather around the kitchen table in the evening and swap tales of the time the river got so high you could see under it, or about the lamb that was so long-legged it looked like a rattlesnake on stilts.

In high school, his interest grew when he heard Henrietta Child, the walking storyteller of Appalachia who was in her eighties when he was still a high school student at Berea College Foundation School in Kentucky. There were stories around the campfire and on five student trips to Europe.

Grown up, he became a minister and many stories were sermons. For 18 years Hutchinson served as a chaplain at the University of Nebraska and a Fellow in UNL's Centennial Education program. It took years to learn to write using the same guidelines he gives for good oral storytelling in his 1985 book *Storytelling Tips.*

"Don't say 'a man,'" Hutchinson advises. "Talk about how he walks with a cane, his hand trembling, taking short steps and plopping into his seat. You want to show rather than tell."

Storytelling--or a written story--usually starts with a character the audience can care about, the author says. Do this, he suggests, by presenting the smells, touch, sound and feel of what's happening to the character.

While Hutchinson spends most of the school year telling stories to school children and adult groups for a living, his summers are devoted to writing. In addition to *Storytelling Tips,* he has written *Doc Graham: Sandhills Doctor* (1970), *Images of Mary* (1971), *Exon: Biography of a Governor* (1973), and *Savidge Brothers: Sandhill Aviators* ,(1982).

Duane Hutchinson, Storyteller
(Used with permission)

From *Savidge Brothers*

INTRODUCTION

West of our farm in Northeast Nebraska lay a fabled, mystery-locked land called "The Goose Lake Country." Near there the Savidge Brothers flew the first airplanes anywhere around. My father spoke of it in hushed tones.

"The lake is shaped like a wild goose," he said. "The Canadas stop there in the spring and fall. There are deep grass meadows and places where water shoots out of the ground. In pastures some natural fountains rise higher than your head."

I tried to imagine a fountain without any railing around it. I couldn't.

"The trees grow tall in that country," said my father, "because they have their feet in water."

I pictured trees with feet, with wet shoes.

Sturdy pioneers lived in Goose Lake Country, he explained. The Savidge brothers from Ewing (he pronounced it "you'ing") built the first airplane anywhere in the country, almost--built it right in the barn on the old Savidge Ranch. They flew over our farm once, back in the 'teens.

The first flying machine! Magic towns lay beyond our cornfields to the west, towns like Chambers where trees grew in the street and Amelia where artesian water flowed in every house without help from anybody. In Ewing, only ten miles north of this Savidge place, a ghostly woman with a white dress floated through town at night. And not far from Goose Lake was a real ghost town. Even the name of the town was known only to the chosen few who knew the country well--Deloit. I could never say that name without a whisper, the way I said *hocus pocus.*

During the summer of 1935 our cornfields turned brown in July. Dust choked our noses and cut apart our curtains. One day my father announced we would go to Goose Lake Country. So, we loaded our robin's-egg-blue Durant with a picnic basket and an ice cream freezer. (We had kept the ice buried deep in straw underground since the winter before.)

How I loved the Durant with its ivory speedometer panel and marble gearshift handle! When Dad put on his Stetson hat and Mom wore the hat with the red cosmos on the front, we knew we were going somewhere special.

We drove west past burned fields. Grasshoppers jumped from the side of the road and bounced off the windows. As I stood up in the back seat between my big sister Rilva and my brother Elvin, who was almost as big as she was, I watched the red ribbon of grass come toward us between the sandhill car tracks. When I turned around, I watched the sand churning up from the back wheels and the ribbon of grass going away.

"How did the Savidge brothers get started flying?" Elvin asked. He was the scientist.

"Did they read about the Wright Brothers in school?" Rilva asked. She was the teacher.

"You'll meet a man today," my father said, "who can answer those questions. He lived in the Savidge home for many years."

"Oh, Toady! " I yelled. Father had told stories about Toady as long as I could remember.

From *Doc Graham, Sandhills Doctor*

I was snapped from my reverie as Doc's story romped to its climax. His own erupting laughter almost obliterated his last words. We were all caught in the excitement and humor of the picture he had drawn out of his own vast experience. Laughter was the release of the tensions of the day. It was good to be together, to re-live again a little of what was being lost from the past.

"Doc," I pleaded with sudden inspiration, "could we sit down together some time and have you tell some stories for my tape recorder? I'm afraid the time is going to come . . . well, like with my father, when these things are going to be lost."

A worried, yet pleased, look came into his eyes. I knew that he was thinking about his heavy burden of work with patients scattered in two rural counties. And perhaps he was thinking about the impersonality of the machine. His stories were for people.

"You ought to catch him down in the pool hall late at night," one of the farmers suggested with a sly grin. "That's when you hear the stories."

This observation brought more laughter from the group. Here was part of the enigma of Dr. Graham--a man who would exhaust himself with his practice, yet loved sociable company and non-professional banter so much that he was continually on the prowl for various escapes. The bowling alley, the pool hall, the fire station just through the block back of his house; these were some of his favorite haunts.

"Nina Belle Graham has walked more miles looking for her husband than anybody else in town," someone once told me. "Yes, and when she came in the front door, he scooted out the back door," someone else added. "He knew she had a phone call for him to go twenty miles to give somebody a remedy."

Yet the husband-wife, doctor-nurse team, lived through the years in remarkable harmony. Thanks probably to her patience and her ability to participate in his lively wit they shared a zest for life. Her experiences added to his and made good telling too.

"It's the *people* that have made these years interesting," Nina Belle told me later. "It is the characters we have had here in Elgin and out in the Sandhills. And believe me, we have had some unusual ones!"

Duane Hutchinson photo by Red, IA *Express*

SHIRLEY LUETH 'DIDN'T PLAN TO WRINKLE'-- OR TO WRITE ABOUT IT

She claimed she could do a good job on floors, windows and newspaper columns--but even so the *Aurora News Register* got more than they bargained for when they hired Shirley Lueth.

Almost immediately her "Prayer and Peanut Butter" column, featuring her husband, seven children, precocious dog and her nemesis neighbor (Perfect Shirley with shiny floors and a husband who only smoked on the porch), became a big hit.

Also in the *Grand Island Independent* since 1974, the column is now syndicated as far away as Texas and Illinois.

The papers received so many requests for back issues of columns that *Prayer and Peanut Butter*, a collection of those columns, became her first book. After a first printing of 5,000 copies, the book went on to 15 more printings.

Writing came about by economic "chance," Lueth says. "We had three children at the University of Nebraska-Lincoln and another one with her hand in our wallets ready to go when my husband suggested a part-time job for me might help get us seven college educations."

Until then, Lueth's only writing was letters to friends. A college art major at Southern Illinois University, she had planned to go to Greenwich Village-- until marriage and seven children came along.

"Writing's too easy," Lueth claims. "I even laugh out loud when I'm doing it. I write about what I know, and I know what makes a family go. It's all based on truth--and a bit of exaggeration."But "easy" work is a religiously kept writing schedule of 9 a.m. to noon every day. She keeps a nightly journal and takes a notebook with her wherever she goes. It's meant giving up sunshine, bridge, and coffee with friends, Lueth said.

And, to promote her work, she goes and goes and goes--all over the United States on speaking engagements. She has an agent to keep up with the books and magazine articles--recent ones appeared in *McCall's* and *Writer's Magazine*, for example.

Her husband now works full-time on the business end of her books and operates the Lueth House Publishing Co. which takes care of what she calls the "bathroom books" (you read a little bit at a time, here and there) between the New York-published major books.

The second book, *I Didn't Plan to be a Witch*, published by Avon books, is more than a popular success. The Minnesota school system uses it in school guidance counselors' offices to help students learn how to communicate better with parents. *Bubble, Bubble Toil and Trouble* and her newest book, *Look Out! I'm Peeking in Your Window* continue her humorous look at a family growing up and moving out of the house, leaving the furniture and dog and old folks to growl at each other.

Lueth says she is not above mentioning the "unmentionables," which is the case with her book due out next year: *I Didn't Plan to Wrinkle!*

From *Watch Out!! I'm Peeking in Your Window!*

"NO ONE WILL EVER CONFESS"

A deep mystery to parents is how to solve the problem of "Who's to Blame?"

It's easy enough when you walk into a room and the kid has meringue on his upper lip. He's the one who took the slice out of the lemon pie.

At our house, however, I always found the pie had disappeared but everyone had clean lips. When I curled both fists into the air and yelled "Okay, who ate the pie?" our oldest son swore he hadn't had a bite of food for two days.

"I'm starving," he said quietly, "but I'd never ever touch your pie, dear mama." Obviously he'd folded his angel wings beneath his T-shirt. I couldn't see them but surely they were there.

"I'm on a diet," a teenaged daughter confided. "I don't eat sweets." I wondered to myself who was putting the candy wrappers in her dresser drawer. I didn't say anything. I didn't want to be the one responsible for warping her tender mind.

"I'd never do that without permission," another angelic voice whispered. She was practically flying through the air with pure innocence.

"I bet a tramp came in the back door and got it" our youngest child said seriously. "They do that on television." I didn't even bother explaining that in this day and age, tramps no longer snitch pies but prefer stereos, silverware and strong boxes.

My husband claims trying to discover the blame is the hardest part of being a parent. "No one will ever confess." he sighed. "If just once someone would stand right up, look me in the eye and say 'I did it, dad', I'd go to my grave happy. What did George Washington's father have that I don't have?"

A wig, fancy farm and a potential president I told him.

Our children have outnumbered us for years. Once we were equal. Once we had two little girls and two big parents. Even then it was hard. Oh, it worked out swell when one was 14 months old and the other two weeks. We knew right away the tiny infant in the bassinet hadn't jumped up and dumped over the potted plant. But our toddler gave it the old college try. She set the mold. She gave 'passing the buck' a dirty name.

"Baby did it," she said sincerely when I asked my first silly mother's question..."Who made this mess?" I think she actually believed it.

As pre-schoolers they had no qualms about placing the blame on someone else. "Augie pooped in my pants," our three-year-old son came to me walking funny and with a surprised look on his face. "Bad doggie."

"Mary Poppins was here dusting and broke this vase, Mommy," our little daughter said primly. Isn't that awful?"

As they outgrow bizarre alibis, they moved to flesh and blood realistic ones. Each other. "It had to be her," a brother pointed to a sister. "I was 3,000 miles away when daddy's electric razor blew up."

"Don't look at me," our daughter said when I showed her my brand new expensive lipstick snapped at the stem. She turned to her brother. "He's the one who will eat anything."

Gradually, however, as they became older they formed a strong coalition. Not only did they stop admitting to personal crimes, they wouldn't squeal on each other. If a fight broke out in the playroom...no one started it. According to them, it happened by osmosis. The grunts, small slaps and stomping feet could reach a fevered pitch but let me ask who was to blame for the fight and calm settled like a warm blanket.

"We're not fighting," a son gasped between chipped teeth. "We were only playing." He threw a friendly arm around his brother's bruised shoulders and limping away together they looked back to see if I was still watching. If I was in sight, they smiled and held hands. If not...grunts, small slaps and stomping feet echoed down the hallway.

Once in awhile, though, I demanded justice be served. Such was the case of the mysterious disappearance of the PTA Easter Doughnuts.

That year, when straws were drawn during the previous meeting of our PTA, I had lost the drawing, and "volunteered" to chair the school's annual spring Easter Tea. Two other mothers were appointed to serve with me. We were the committee. "We might be small...but we're mighty," I promised as I bowed among the handclaps of the relieved members who had won the draw. "We'll have a grand tea this year."

According to one on the committee she worked 24 hours a day away from home and the other had migraines. "I'll do what I can to help during my coffee break," the working mommy said tiredly.

"If I can open my eyes for five minutes without fainting, you can count on me to fold napkins," the other offered in an aching voice. Together they said "You aren't busy. You do it."

It wasn't really that hard. I simply ordered ten dozen yellow and green frosted doughnuts and asked if they could be sprinkled with bright glittering stars. "No problem," the baker said and had them ready days in advance of the tea. I picked them up from the bakery and they were beautiful. Placing three long boxes in the freezer I called the school principal to tell her everything was under control. "I'm glad," she said. "This is our last event of the school year. It's important things go smoothly."

Did they go smoothly? Or did a tramp come and steal them all? Read on and find out.

(From *Watch Out! I"m Peeking In Your Window* . Copyright 1986 by Shirley Lueth. Used with permission of author.)

ROBERT T. REILLY WRITES WITH THE LUCK OF THE IRISH

Robert Reilly weaves into and out of his narrative like an Irish storyteller, which he is. Speaking in a soft voice, he appears laid back and calm. But don't let that exterior fool you. He's all business when it comes to writing, and he's a very exacting task master--especially on himself.

Fourteen years ago Reilly was president and partner of an Omaha advertising agency which bore his name. UNO came and asked him to teach in its journalism school. After some consideration, Reilly said "yes" because it would give him the opportunity to write, which is what he likes to do best.

The change in jobs, however, cost him about 60% in salary cut. Married and the father of ten children, Reilly knew he'd need more than a college professor's salary to live on. He determined how much he needed and set that as a goal for how much writing he would do and sell each year.

Writing is not new to Reilly. He had a journalism degree from Boston University, had edited a service newspaper, "wrote bad poetry," and eventually came to Creighton University in Omaha to head its public relations department.

He began selling regularly in 1954, and in 1957 sold his first book.

Reilly says "An artist needs some tension in his life. For a writer that tension can only be relieved by writing."

"I didn't intend to do textbooks," he says, "but I am now revising three that I wrote in the first place."

Textbook revisions aren't his favorite kind of writing. As we talked, the phone rang several times from publishers wanting to know when his revisions would be in the mail.

His office floor had several stacks of papers and books--one stack for each book to come. His office window overlooks a breathtaking view of the North Hills.

Reilly figures to teach one more year, then retire to full-time writing. Now he writes 30-35 hours a week, in addition to the teaching and related activities which take up about 55 hours. "But I'm always thinking about writing."

With 10 books published, three of which are textbooks ("they pay well"), Reilly's plans always include a book every other year, one article per month ("most of them are contracted for, only three or four are looking for a home"), and four television or movie scripts per year--documentaries or promotion pieces.

74

Reilly says there are still lots of markets for writers. "Use your own marketing savvy. Ask yourself, "Could I write for this market? Could I write for that market?'"

He also advises ,"initiate a contact." Reilly should know. He's written for more than 100 national magazines in the 35 years he's been a freelance writer.

He loves interviewing. "I may interview 50 or 60 people for one article, even if it's only 3,500 words. People talk to me, and I share something with them." He takes his notes on a pocket-sized note pad, because he can carry that with him. "Journalistic background helps you wait for the one great line-- somebody else can always say it better than you can," he concludes.

From *Come Along to Ireland*

Those who named Ireland "The Emerald Isle" didn't overstate the case. When the mists have lifted and the quaint villages fade and the castle ruins are forgotten, it's a memory of green that remains. On a single hill one might glimpse greens the color of early apples, ripe olives, or aging moss, all interlaced like tweed with low rock walls for seams. Here and there some yellow furze, or red holly berries, blackthorn hedges or golden stacks of wheat, or a tree twisted in the Atlantic wind.

Even in the rain, Ireland is a beautiful country and, when the sun follows rain, it sparkles as if newly minted.

(From *Come Along to Ireland*. Copyright, 1980, by Robert T. Reilly. Used with permission by author.)

From *Red Hugh, Prince of Donegal*

In the far west of Donegal, where the waters of Lake Eske plunge headlong into the Atlantic, a solitary castle stood guard over a quiet September. Shaped like a sledge it was, with the massive head facing the stream and the long row of stone dwellings forming a handle that stretched to the opposite wall. Low-lying heather and tiny furze dotted the courtyard and repeated the triangular patttern which marked the gabled rooftops. The fortress-like head rose four stories high and towered abo ve the rest of the buildings. Each corner was the base for a turret and the largest of these faced the ocean. There were few windows and these were but wide enough to accommodate the archers.

Red Hugh, Prince of Donegal. Farrar Straus and Giroux, copyright 1966. Used with permission of the author.

CAPTAIN NEBRASKA MAKES HISTORY
A LAUGHING MATTER

Later Roger Welsch would become known as folk hero Captain Nebraska, folklore scholar Dr. Welsch, professor of English and anthropology at the University of Nebraska-Lincoln, and the only Lincoln author t o joke that he's been nominated for inclusion in the Vatican's 1984 Index of Prohibited Books. But that's not the way the legend began back in the late '60s, the heyday of "folkniks," Welsch will tell folks in the evenings at his post at the big table at the Silver Dollar Bar in rural Dannebrog where he spends time swapping true life adventures "to get material" for his next five books.

The mustachioed author prof, who makes sure his best blue and white denim pin-striped suit has all three brass rivet side buttons up and the bib snapped for public engagements, has bcome, in his own words, "a real hot property."

He claims that his own personal legend began as a coffeehouse singer around Colorado and Wyoming doing Nebraska folksongs in summers off from teaching German and English literature.

The folk music helped him decide to attend an Indiana University Folklore Institute where he ran across old W. P. A. photos and articles from Depression days. "Here's material that should be published, I thought. And boom! I was hooked."

Before long, Welsch had his hooks into almost everything--Omaha Indian tribal myths, folkways of early Russian-German settlers and Great Plains newcomers, history, music, literature and other "ribald materials."

He says, in his tremendously popular guidebook, *Inside Lincoln*, that he "wound up spending a good part of my life studying, researching, and writing about Plains history after I found out that REAL history involves sex, violence, corruption, crime, and--best of all--lots of laughter."

He regularly dispenses guffaws with the alacrity of the slick patent medicine salesman who could cure things you didn't know ailed you until then, especially the sickness and sin of boredom. Welsch gets about a dozen requests a week to tell his tales. He has a dozen books and hundreds of published stories in everything from prestigious academic journals to humor magazines. He writes a bi-weekly humor column for The*Lincoln Journal*.

Prolificacy notwithstanding, author Welsch says he's not disciplined and works "only on the guilt system. I loaf away all my time, then work like a mad dog to meet the deadline." He says he hates writing, and that it's the hardest work he's ever done in his life, even though he spends every day doing it.

The latest book, *Cather's Kitchen*, co-authored with his wife, Linda, contains actual recipes used in Willa Cather's childhood home. This past year he's also edited *Beautiful Dannebrog*, co-authored *You Know You're a Nebraskan When* with cartoonist Paul Fell, and produced a book with cassette, *Highway to Heritage* with songs and stories to keep folks rolling with laughter as they roll across Nebraska on Interstate 80.

In the works are *Stories from the Big Table* , ribald stories from small town bars, and *You Know You're a Husker When, Son of You Know You're a Nebraskan*, and *You Know You're a Farmer.*

For Welsch, real life's work is laughter--laughter that works, if you're a Nebraskan.

From *Omaha Tribal Myths and Trickster Tales*

Rabbit

The Trickster appears throughout the world folklore and literature in a thousand forms, from a god to a ghost, from a spider to a spirit. In Omaha culture the Trickster appears as a rabbit, as a coyote, and as Ictinike, a strange spirit-man, and in one lone tale as a racoon.

It would be a real delight if I could clearly delineate the character of the Trickster in these different guesses, but just as nature blends with the supernatural in Omaha life, just as animals and man are blended into the one concept of life, the Trickster, too, does not present us with such a clear and obvious set of categories. Rabbit, Ictinike, and Coyote merge at their edges. Bewilderingly, these alternate masks of the same mysterious character even encounter each other in some of these tales and try to outdo each other in roguery. In some cases the same story is told about Rabbit and Coyote, about Coyote and Ictinike. They change forms at will and yet remain always the Trickster.

And yet there are some concentrations of characteristics about the identities of the three major Omaha Trickster figures. I will discuss Ictinike and Coyote Later, where I tell their tales, Ictinike being the most prominent of the taboo violators and Coyote, the fool, the victim of his own perversity.

Rabbit is ever the Trickster, deceptive and naive, clever and stupid, showing all the contradictions that so encourage comparisons with man and god, with the environment of the Omaha tribe. But Rabbit more than the other forms of the Trickster in Omaha tales is two things, the culture hero and a surprise source of courage.

To me this is a powerful and vivid statement of the Omaha sense of irony. The Plains Indian was painfully aware of the contradictions of life. Rabbit, the most timid of Plains animals--"split mouth," "big eyes," "big foot," as he is cursed in the tales, assumed coward even by his grandmother--is the Omaha Prometheus, Odysseus, and Ictharus. This terrified little trembler, we are told in these stories, is a killer of ogres, a capturer of the sun, gives turkeys red eyes, and can be a clever and courageous fighter.

The lesson cannot have been lost on the young Omaha listening to these stories 150 years ago. The Omaha were a small tribe of farmers, faced with the awesome fury of the Plains climate and neighbors like the Cheyenne, Arapaho, Pawnee, and Sioux.

And in retrospect we might ask if this was a vain comparison, a pathetic optimism. Well, the Plains still teem with rabbits, the Nebraska night still trembles with the coyote's aria, and the Omaha are the only Nebraska Indians who remain on their native soil.

From *Inside Lincoln*

IT'S ...THE ARTS

Lincoln has had its share of problems with the arts scene. Lincoln is still a small, rural town about as deep into the boondocks as one can go. It has therefore remained about as far from the Art Scene a la New York and San Francisco as one can get.

Do I lament that? No, I wish there were another thousand miles of prairie on either side of us. But the fact remains that the artsy-fartsy crowd has an upstream canoe trip in Lincoln.

One of the most recent flaps and one I enjoyed immensely was the fuss about the "sculpture" for--where else?--13th and O. The Lincoln art committee was gaga over something submitted by an artist-not-from-Nebraska (which means it has to be good, right?) which he designed to grace 13th and O. It consisted of several massive I-beams to be set corner to corner across the intersection like an unfinished bridge, one vertical member standing plunk in the middle of the intersection.

The Federal Highway folks displayed a terribly gauche lack of culture by suggesting that it might not be a good idea at all--maybe even unwise--to put I-beams in the middle of a Federal highway. The Artsies, not to be denied, had their boy from the East devote a full thirty seconds of creative genius to redesigning his masterpiece. This one, still made of massive I-beams, had monstrous pillars on either side, so if a semi should hit it, it would fall away and crush thirty or forty pedestrians. This design was laughed out of business by the uncultured citizens of Lincoln, most of whom are still trying to figure out when they are going to finish the Co-Op gas station sign on the southwest corner of 12th and O. Presumably the committee is still searching for a means to inflict this emperor's suit on Lincoln.

FLASH! Just as this was going to print, the arts committee again reared its ugly head, or vice versa, and did indeed come up with yet another New York "artist" with yet another $75,000 project. He says that no one will be able to guess what his art-for-O will look like. Bet I can guess. It will look like nothing at all.

FLASH AGAIN! I was dead wrong. The plans for this wonderful new art piece were printed in the Lincoln paper just yesterday and I was mistaken: it does look like something. It looks for all the world like two gigantic pieces of doggie doo-doo. I thought at first that maybe some pranksters had managed to get a parody plan printed in the paper, but no. It's tough to parody folks who are their own parody. So welcome to Lincoln, but be careful not to step in the sculpture.

78

You Know You're a Nebraskan illustrations by Paul Fell. All rights reserved.

BARBARA BONHAM ONE OF 'NON-EXOTIC' BREED

Barbara Bonham thought she couldn't write, because "I thought writers were an exotic breed." Then a woman who wrote confessions moved to Franklin, where Bonham lived. Not only was she a writer, Bonham observed, but she was a person, a mother, and not at all exotic. She encouraged Bonham to write for the confession market, so Bonham wrote her first works at 21, and wrote and wrote for three years--confessions and western romances----before she made her first sale.

That's when she got an agent and continued to write confessions. "They are strongly plotted, and I like to do strong plots. Characterization comes slower," she says. But she feels the latest of her 16 published books has good characterization.

She takes about 14 months to research and write a book. She does library research, plans the outline of the book, then goes to the geographical location of the story. "Plots come after two or three major events are planned," Bonham says, then she does "biographies " of her characters. She doesn't like to write contemporary novels. "I like to write what I like to read," she says.

Bonham writes from nine to three every day. Her friends don't call during those hours, because they know she is working. Most of her books are mass market paperbacks, but she does have a teen book on Willa Cather. After all, Franklin *is* in Cather country.

One of Bonham's romances, *Passion's Price*, (Playboy Press Paperbacks, 1977) made the *New York Times* Paperback Best Seller list. She had a strong physical reaction to that. "I guess I thought it was going to change my life. When I saw that it wasn't going to, I settled down."

She has a juvenile book (10-to-14-year-olds), *Challenge of the Prairie.*, which has been translated into the Thai language. The left hand page is in English, and the right hand page is in Thai. This book and one other of hers are also in German.

Once Bonham finishes a book, she takes three months off. "I may start the research for the next book before I finish the book I'm on." She does not type. "I use a Bic and cheap typing paper. I pay someone to do the typing of the final manuscript." She is developing her latest book, *Bittersweet*, into a trilogy. One of her books, *Green Willow*, is set in Franklin.

From *Wild Harvest*

The late afternoon sun bored in the open windows of the stage - coach, burning Sinda's legs through the emerald green fabric of her skirt. The child on her lap slept soundly, his small body as soft and boneless as a kitten. Leaning her cheek against his fine blonde hair, she gazed pensively at the passing landscape. She was almost home, but it wouldn't be the same.

The Texas brush country flashed by as the driver urged the horses on at full speed. The leaflets of the mesquite and huisache, the feathery leaves of the retama, deceived the observer with their delicacy. Hidden among those leaves were thorns that could rip and tear the clothing and flesh of any rider chasing a longhorn through the chaparral. They were far more wounding than the spines the prickly pear honestly displayed. Scarcely any of the trees and plants that composed the chaparral were thornless. The brush country was forbidding, even sinister, but Sinda loved it.

The landscape was so familiar to her she could judge her distance from home by the roll and crinkle of the earth as it sped by the window. Brown eyes, normally serene, checked off the landmarks one by one. The firm chin resting on the child's fair head was softened by a mouth dimpled at each corner. Skin as translucent as the child's stretched over high cheek - bones, its color bleached by the thick red hair that lay in gleaming waves around her face.

These last two years in Waco had been intellectually stimulating beyond anything she had ever experienced, and she wished desperately that she could return in the fall and finish college, but her father had refused to let her continue. "You've kept Charles waiting long enough. You'll marry him this summer."

Used with permission of the author.

WRITING'S THE 'ONLY WAY' MARNIE ELLINGSON WANTS TO MAKE A LIVING

Marnie Ellingson has always been fascinated by the Regency period in history. She loves reading Jane Austen because "Austen lived in that time, and she's the best." All but one of her seven romance books are about the Regency period.

Ellingson has always loved to read, and she felt that writing was the only way to make a living. "I wasn't quite dumb enough to think I could make a living at it without some sort of training. So I went to Northwestern University and took journalism. I took their magazine sequence with the idea of going to New York City and working on a magazine that used fiction."

But, as in the romances she writes, fate intervened; she married her heart's desire and moved to Omaha instead.

In Omaha she has been writing ever since. Her first big fiction sale was to *Ladies Home Journal*. It was followed by sales to *McCall's, Good Housekeeping, Redbook, Cosmopolitan,* and *Woman's Day*.

"When I first started writing, magazines used 5,000 words in their short stories. Then it became 4,500, then 4,000, and finally 3,500. I got used to telling a story in a short space." So when she decided in 1978 to write a Regency novel, she thought, "Now I have all the room to maneuver, and it's almost more than I can stand."

The decision to write a Regency novel "was like a light going on in my head. I really felt I could do it better . I knew more about the Regency period than some others who were writing about it." So she got busy and by 1980 had sold four.

"Regency novels have a lot of dialogue, which I like to write. They're about 170 to 180 pages long, and there's no sub-plot. They can be funny, and, if well done, they can be very comforting."

Ellingson now writes about one book a year. "I don't believe in writing only when you're inspired. Write whether you're inspired or not." One year she tried writing a contemporary romance. "I've never finished it," she says.

She works in longhand. "I used to write in the orthodontist's office, at children's dancing lessons, late at night when the typing might wake the family. I got used to working in longhand." When she's done with the writing, she puts it together on the computer in her office.

Ellingson has written continuously, with the exception of a short time when her children were small. The explosion in the romance field and the death of one of her favorite Regency writers got her back on track. "This year I'm trying a mystery. It's a learning experience. I'm having trouble with the action," she states.

"I would love to write great literature," says Ellingson. "But that's not my talent. We have to work with the talent we have."

From *Dolly Blanchard's Fortune*

CLIO LANGDON SWEPT a red-gold curl off her forehead, heedless of her carefully dressed hair, and declared, "I vow, If you had been at the Blakeleys' rout last night and seen Melisande deLacey dancing with Richard, you'd have wept buckets."

Her sister, on the sofa opposite, merely stared at her, but the young lady in the window seat lifted clear grey eyes from the tapestry she was working and enquired mildly, "Why? Did he tread on her toes?"

"Oh, I should think that unlikely," Miss Cassandra Langdon said. Don't you remember when Mama hired the dancing master to teach us, Richard was always the first to learn the steps? I should think it much more likely that Melisande might tread on *his* toes, though why that should make us weep I don't know, for I hardly think it would hurt him. She is so slender she can't weigh very much, and she would only be wearing kid slippers or perhaps Denmark satin, while Richard--"

"Oh, Cassie, do stop prattling on about people's feet being trod on. Dolly was only being droll. You are so prosy-minded," her sister Clio said.

"Then why should we have wept?" Cassie asked.

"They make such a perfect couple," her sister sighed. "Melisande is so very fair with that golden hair and those midsummer-sky blue eyes, and her skin is like peach bloom with such a delicate blush, while Richard is so dark and handsome, and when they look at each other it's--it's as if you could hear coralbells ringing."

"Coralbells?" Dolly said. "Gracious, that does sound serious."

"But of course they are doomed," Clio said, sighing again.

"Indeed?" Dolly asked. "I can see I have been away so long I am out of touch. What is the nature of their particular doom? Surely neither has contracted a fatal disease?"

"Oh, do be serious. It's worse than that!" Clio told her.

Dolly looked startled. "What could be worse than a fatal disease?"

"Poverty," Clio declared.

"Oh, I'm sure you must be wrong," Dolly assured her. "At least I should think so. While I have not had the misfortune to suffer from either case, I wouldcertainly a great rather be poor than fatally ill."

"Oh, Dolly, sometimes I think you haven't a romantic bone in your body. Can't you imagine what an affecting picture it would make, to lie on a sofa growing paler and paler while your lover knelt at your side weeping with grief and tearing out his hair in a distracted frenzy?"

(from *Dolly Blanchard's Fortune*. Walker and Company. Copyright 1983. Used with permission of the author.)

Ellingson photo by Donald Jack Studios.

THE WORLD NOTICED WHEN CATHERINE KIDWELL CREATED 'THE WOMAN I AM'

Catherine Kidwell didn't plan to make history--or even to change her lifestyle--when she started back to college at the University of Nebraska-Lincoln as a freshman art major a few years ago.

But for the now-famous novelist, whose book, *Dear Stranger*, has been on Top Ten best seller lists across the country the last two years, nothing in her life has been the same.

Like her novel's heroine, Kidwell finds herself in an exciting new world.

After earning a bachelor of fine arts degree, Kidwell went on to become the first person ever to write a novel as a creative thesis for a Master of Arts degree in English at UNL. She also became the first to publish the thesis simultaneously in the U.S. and Great Britain. In addition, the work has been serialized in a British magazine, translated into Swedish, and produced in a large print edition. Excerpts from her book aired on the NBC, Mutual and RKO networks.

Warner Books spent $100,000 promoting the blockbuster novel as a "new genre" of romantic fiction. Kidwell was given a red-carpet tour, appearing on television and radio talk shows across the nation.

But the book is far from the Harlequin Books style usually thought of by the term "romance novel." Set in Lincoln over a 30-year period beginning during World War II, the novel is partly autobiographical. "But," she adds, "I didn't do everything Bonnie (the book's heroine) does."

Dear Stranger is the expanded version of her thesis, which is in print as *The Woman I Am*. Both books tell the story of a secretary who fell in love with a soldier she met in the ballroom of the (thinly disguised) Cornhusker Hotel in Lincoln. Bonnie marries him three days later, divorces him, and then meets him again 30 years and a second marriage later. *Dear Stranger* explores the relationships between men and women at mid-life.

In Kidwell's novels, women deal with the complex feelings of loneliness and how they try to fulfill those needs in the way they react with older people. She says it is a positive message.

It is that statement, that youthful romance can also be part of being 50 years old, that gives *Dear Stranger* the "feminist romance" label sometimes applied to it, the author says.

Her latest book is a how-to-write book: *I Couldn't Put It Down: How to Write Quality Fiction in 10 Easy Lessons.* It uses examples from *The Woman I Am* and *Dear Stranger*. A new novel, which also centers around the old Cornhusker Hotel, is in progress.

Her own dream, Kidwell admits, was never to be a novelist. "That just happened along the way of being a student."

From *Dear Stranger*

A mantle of crystal had settled over the city. Freezing mist veiled the near and obscured the distant. Winter twilight vanquished color. Diamond trees lined platinum streets. The sidewalk stretched into a flat ribbon of ice.

Noise would shatter the brittle air. She whispered, "So beautiful. Oh, it's beautiful."

John dropped the suitcase. He rounded the end of the sidewalk with a few steps. Bonnie's squeal violated the silence as, arms spread for banking, he slid down the declining walk parallel to the street, skillfully guiding himself onto the grass at the bottom of the incline.

She shrieked again and laughed. "You're crazy--going the wrong way."

"Who's crazy?" he shouted. "You can't slide uphill."

She took a few cautious steps to the turn in the sidewalk and spread out her arms. "Catch me. Here I come."

Her jerky running start turned into a lurching slalom. The boots weren't made for sliding but she managed to keep upright all the way down into John's outstretched arms.

Without consultation, they climbed up the frozen grass and slid down the walk again together.

"Shall we press our luck?" he panted.

"Why not?"

This time they almost didn't make it, Bonnie clutching wildly at his steady, strong arm. Their gasps exploded into laughter, bounding into a picture postcard world.

"If you think that's good, wait till we put on our skates," John said.

They climbed back up the incline and she waited for him to retrieve her bag before they threaded their way across the grass in the other direction.

"You'll like our lodge in the Adirondacks. Know how to ski?"

She shook her head. "But I can learn."

"You'll be great. I can't wait to teach you."

She looked around. "Think there's anybody else out there?"

She looked carefully, pointing through the haze across the street. "Up in that tree, there's an old man in a pointed cap and cowboy boots. He's the only one."

She stopped and cupped her hands around her mouth. "Hey, old man," she called, "did you know this is my wedding night?"

"I don't think he heard you."

She raised her hands again, shouting, "Hey, old man--"

"I'll help. *Hey--*"

Bonnie pulled back on his arm. "John," she said, "we're lunatics."

"Momma and Poppa Lunatic, talking about a future."

"Oh, tell me there's a future."

"I promise. Thirty years from now you'll be a gentle old lady in a . shawl with our grandchildren gathered around you saying, 'Tell me about your wedding during the big war, Granma.'"

She smiled. "And you'll be an old man in a pointed cap and cowboy boots sitting up in a tree spying on lovers."

They were the only passengers on the bus. The diminutive driver kept her attention riveted on the icy pavement, skillfully easing the big vehicle up to stop signs and around corners.

Downtown, the few people on the street eased by like ghosts. Out of the mist the gray stone church loomed like a deserted Gothic castle. They rounded the corner, past the steep stone steps, to see a light shining through the small stained-glass windows of the chapel. Like a candle in the window at home, it drew them to the less imposing side entrance. They held each other up one last time on the stone steps, and stood tall again with firm footing in the dry hallway.

The hall was chilly, but when they passed through the heavy chapel doors, warmer air touched their stiff faces and fingers. Mellowed wood paneled the walls here, and the deep red carpet echoed the somber colors of stained-glass windows with night on the other side. Light was hushed by the amber bulbs in the antique chandelier, and the low-flamed candles in the brass candelabra.

A small man with thinning hair and glasses came toward them, his hand outstretched to grasp Bonnie's.

"Here you are, my dear. Wretched night out there."

She was grateful for his warm handclasp, and turned to introduce John. Dr. Miller examined the bridegroom.

"Glad to meet you. I know Bonnie will have chosen a good man."

"Thank you, sir," John replied.

"We're a little late," Bonnie said. "You'll be late for your meeting."

Dr. Miller shook his head. "Doesn't matter, they can start without me. This is more important."

Two persons stood close to the altar. Bonnie recognized the fuzzy round figure of the church secretary, but she wasn't sure who the man was.

They left their coats and the leather bag at the back of the room, then had to detour around the silent electric organ to join the others up front. With linked hands, they walked down the aisle together. She looked for sadness in the silent organ, the empty benches, the strangers at the altar, the stormy night. Joy kept breaking through instead.

They paced their steps together and reached the end of their a capella processional with grace. Their attendants stood on either side and Dr. Miller beamed at them, Bible in hand.

"Bonnie and John," he said solemnly, "I would like for you to meet Miss Stapleton and Mr. Chap."

The older people all wore rimless glasses with little nose pieces cutting into the flesh. Miss Stapleton's glasses were smudged. Mr. Chap's coat didn't match his trousers. Bonnie wished she could remember where she had seen him before.

Dr. Miller cleared his throat. "Shall we begin?"

(From *Dear Stranger* . Warner Books. Copyright 1984. Used with permis - sion of the author.)

Kidwell Photo by Gary Buehler.

SIX MILLION PUBLISHED WORDS—AND WAYNE LEE'S STILL AT IT

Wayne Lee didn't take his first writing assignment seriously. After all, the high school English teacher said to write about an impossible experience. So Lee wrote a wild adventure about a kid who pulled up what looked like an ordinary garden weed and found himself transported to another planet.

When his teacher told him to report to the classroom after school, Wayne Lee recalls, "I was sure I was going to catch it." But the teacher told him he had a knack for storytelling he should develop.

Meanwhile, there was farming, and the need to make a living in Western Nebraska. It took a "good many years before I tried publishing," Lee said. He started his spare-time writing by doing "a lot of sports stuff. I'm a sports nut," Lee confesses. "But it's like the feller raising wheat--you do what sells."

One of Lee's early books was called *The Wild Towns of Nebraska*. "But then I found out they were mostly all wild towns back then," Lee said. "I sure had to pull in my horns to include just two of everything--two railroad towns, for example, two trails, two ranch towns."

Immediately the western adventure stories sold well--but then so did more than 650 short stories and serials, six million words in all. He's written juvenile stories, mysteries for kids, and literally dozens of western adventure stories. His books have been translated into six or seven languages.

The prolific author has been named Nebraska historian of the year and is listed in both *Who's Who in America* and *Who's Who in the World*. He is a friend of Western author Louis L'Amour and wrote the introduction for one of his classics.

Lee is completing his 53rd full-length book--he writes two every winter in Texas where he and his wife retreat for a few months. "It just seems like I write all the time," he says. "I start at 5 a.m. and stop at noon. Afternoons I work in the garden. I write fast. That way there's less correcting to do. And I put in action, lots of action."

He advises young writers to "just work your head off. Do your research. Don't put a repeating rifle into an early West tale. It makes my hair curl. Get your research right--no matter what kind it is."

Most writers don't fail because they can't write, Lee thinks. "They just fail to remember that if you expect writing to give you a living, then you have to work at it like a business. Even now, every day, I punch that clock."

From *War on Nugget Creek*

Dan York looked across the creek toward the ranch. "I'd better get my chore done." He clucked to the team.

"I wouldn't advise it," Trillingham shouted after him.

York wasn't advising it for himself, either, but this was his mission. Besides, Carlita was up there. A third of the money that the store and home of Tom and Renetta York had brought at the sale was Carlita's share. Today he'd deliver her money to her.

It didn't take the wagon long to cross the distance to the ranch. The three riflemen had followed as far as Nugget and stopped, apparently convinced that Dan was going to carry out his mission.

York's approach was noticed by the people at the Box F. Dan saw two men come from the barn to join the man who had come out on the porch of the house. They had all moved out to the yard by the time he reached them. Obviously, the Box F didn't receive many visitors.

Dan quickly picked out Sam Frake. He was even bigger than Jeff Frake and the two shared the same features except that the father's eyes were midnight black instead of brown. A sense of power radiated from him. He stepped out ahead of the others like a stallion ready to meet a challenge.

Dan quickly flashed his eyes over the other two men. There was a sharp conrast between them. The red-headed one with light blue eyes would have been a big man anywhere except standing beside Sam Frake. The other man was small and as colorless as a desert dune, his hair sandy, his eyes gray. His cheeks were sallow in spite of work that surely kept him outside a great deal. The prominent feature that York noticed was the long hooked nose. On his small face, that stood out like a lighthouse on a beach.

"What brings you here?" Frake demanded gruffly.

York stood up in the wagon. "I stopped in Goldtown yesterday," he said. "A young man there picked a fight with me. I shot him."

Sam Frake only glared at York. "What's that to me?" he demanded.

"They told me his name was Jeff Frake. I've got his body here."

Sam Frake's face twisted as if a mule had kicked him in the stomach. The next instant, his hand shot to his gun like lightning.

'POOR JUDY' WRITES
RICH ROMANCE

Who'd have thought pithy "Poor Judy" was a pseudonym for a romantic novelist?

Not even the author of both, Judith Nelson, whose penchant for newsprint was intitially overcome by a desire to escape from a heavy master's thesis in journalism with lighthearted creative writing.

"Just for fun, I wrote the kind of thing I read just for fun," admits Nelson, who fulltime produces brochure and promotional copy for communication services of the University of Nebraska-Lincoln Division of Continuing Studies.

"Poor Judy's Almanac" has been dishing out tongue-in-cheek advice through the *North Platte Telegraph* and Kansas newspapers for 10 years.

Her first romantic fling, literarily speaking, arrived almost by the same kind of accident that regularly befalls her novels' heroines. While on a mission to sell a "serious" novel about newspapering days in western Nebraska, Nelson happened to mention to an agent that she had this little romance smouldering in a box in her closet.

A week out of the closet and the check for the book was in the mail, along with a promotional copy that called Nelson "a sparkling, new talent with great promise." *A Merry Chase* was published in 1985. Warner sent her a handsome advance for her second book, *Kidnap Confusion*, due out in 1986, even before they saw the last half of the book.

Nelson's characters live in the same period in England as those of Jane Austen. Her women are saucy, smart, and not easily smitten by dukes in carriages as by fine-bred horsmanship and the high shenanigans of real wit. It's purple passion with a price. And the price, for Nelson, is laughter-- considered an indiscretion among the proper Regency ladies, but an indispensible asset for Nelson's modern-day readers.

Though she writes every day, alternating daytime academic copy with weekend newspaper column humor and nightly romance writing, Nelson claims there's only one reason anybody writes: "You feel so good when you stop."

"It's plain hard work," she says. "Unless you know you have to push on and do it to feel okay inside, don't bother."

Nelson said that even as a child she "always made up stories." People's response to those was: "Be a teacher" or "Be a nurse."

It's hard to know when you've "arrived" at being a writer, this writer thinks. "It's more of a process of becoming."

As she struggles with daily deadlines and growing into her new role as novelist, Nelson says she frequently thinks of the opening lines from the Robert Frost poem:

"Two roads diverged and I . . .took the one less traveled by . . . And that has made all the difference."

From *The Merry Chase*

If Pettigrew's purpose at that moment was to discomfit the room's two occupants, he succeeded admirably. The lady, who had been rather pale when he first opened the door, flushed rosily and retreated further under the covers until only her head was visible. The gentleman, whose complexion was already high, turned positively florid, his brow darkening. Not only was he pardonably annoyed at having his proposal so rudely interrupted, he was even more angered to find that the interrupter was "that fellow Pettigrew, damn his impudence."

"Sir, you interrupt," Percival said coldly, straightening from his position over Matty and drawing himself to his full height. Even then he was at a remarkable disadvantage in Pettigrew's presence.

"Well, thank goodness for that," Matty snapped. She glared at Percival, then at Pettigrew, noting with growing dismay that just behind the second gentleman was an open-mouthed Aunt Hester. Uttering a groan, Matty wryly reflected that it had been a most unsatisfactory day.

"My betrothed and I wish to be alone," Percival continued haughtily, and Matty stared at him aghast.

"Percy, do stop this nonsense," she begged. "We are not betrothed. I have told you we would not suit. Go away."

But Percival, finding his love's eyes fixed upon him just as Pettigrew looked amused and his aunt indignant, was beyond turning back. Grabbing the hand with which Matty clutched the blankets to her chin, he fell romantically to one knee beside her bed, beginning an impetuous speech which she listened to in open-mouthed amazement. Caesar, who had entered with Pettigrew and Hester, took instant exception to such behavior and barked loudly, then fixed his teeth in Percy's coat and began pulling the man away from his mistress.

(From *The Merry Chase.* Warner Books. Copyright 1985. Used with permis - sion of author.)

THE 'WRITER'S MYSTIQUE' LURED BETH SCHREMPP

"There's a mystique about writers," says Beth Schrempp. "When you say you're a writer, people say in awe, 'You're a writer?' and step back with great respect."

Schrempp is the author of three books, the best of which, even according to her, is *Whisper, Whisper*, which has been translated into German. All of her books have been written under the pseudonym Katherine Court. Even her latest book, a murder mystery about brides being killed on their wedding day, is being written by Katherine Court.

The choice of a pseudo - nym was not hers, but an agent's. He thought she needed a "dignified name" to write adult books.

Schrempp says she's hooked on writing books, although this new one will be her first since 1978. She works with an agent in New York City.

Her first sale, on the first try out, was to *Family Circle* magazine for $500. "It was the worst thing that could have happened," she said. "I was saying, 'Oh, gee, let's buy a house!' There was this wave of confidence that I could do this again and again. I didn't understand the market, though. I happened to send it to just the right magazine at just the right time. It was two years before I sold a second article. The whole thing was a very humbling experience."

Schrempp came to Omaha from St. Joseph, Missouri, to attend Duchesne College. She went on to earn a degree in librarianship at the University of Denver. It was while working in libraries that she learned how to do reearch.

She believes in accuracy of detail. "If your story has a fire in it, call the fire department and find out what happens when a fire is reported. If one of your characters ends up in jail, call the police department and find out how it works." Her latest book has a lot of action set in a florist shop. "I'm a third generation florist, so I know what I'm writing about."

Dialogue comes easy for Schrempp, as do the characters. "I search in my mind for characters. I walk through my mind and find characters to put in my book. I'll see a person I don't know and it will bother the heck out of me until I put him in the book. Once I met this black priest, a good looking and terribly earnest man. I kept saying, 'No, you don't belong in this book.' But he kept showing up in my mind. Finally, I almost said aloud, 'You belong in my next book, don't you?' He smiled and disap - peared. He became Jesse Booter in *Whisper, Whisper*."

Although the majority of her material is made up, there are incidents from her life that appear. But, she warns writers, "Don't fiction-alize real life. Writing fction is not like writing real life."

From *Whisper, Whisper*

"Your Excellency," his seminarian chauffeur touched his arm. "There is barely time now--" He pointed to his watch.

The Bishop looked at him and turned back to the door of the sanctuary. The long banner on the mobile swung in slow serenity.

A hundred years--St. Marks had time. A butterfly floated in a screenless window. Butterflies had time. The congregation sat. The congregation had time.

Everyone and everything had time but Patrick J. Devlin. He moved to a Bishop's business by the clock, by the calendar. He was as scheduled, he thought suddenly, "as a blasted operating room."

Deep down in his Celtic heritage something stirred, something rang, faint but clear. A clarion call to rebellion.

"Just this once--" He made up his mind. "Cancel my ticket on United. Tell Billingsley at the Cathedral that I require his private plane. Now. Gassed up, or whatever they do. And his pilot. Have them wait. Move!"

The seminarian moved.

The Bishop turned to Tuck. "I'm not going to miss this," he said firmly. "Perhaps a chair?"

There were, of course, no chairs. They had all been moved into the church.

Agnes offered her rocker.

The Bishop placed it for a prime view through the sacristy door, and settled himself with satisfaction.

"Now, he said, "I'm going to sit and savor my Episcopal clout."

"Say," he leaned forward a bit. "That young black at the main door--the lavendar cap--"

"Linus," said Tuck.

"We've met," said the Bishop. "And the lady at the side door?"

"Mrs. Zawelski," said Tuck.

"Rugs and peanut butter," said the Bishop. "The rectory, I presume, is covered?"

"Agnes," said Tuck.

"Formidable woman," said the Bishop.

He was suddenly and highly enjoying himself. "To see a parish this united--"

The minutes passed. The elms whispered. The mobile stirred. The butterfly left. The people sat. The Bishop rocked.

Then it happened. There was a shriek and a whoop. And Linus came cartwheeling down the center aisle. "He comin', he comin'," he screeched in front of the altar and cartweeled back.

"Remarkable," said the Bishop.

"Pat--" helplessly from the Pastor. The Bishop spared him a look. "Have you forgotten?" he asked benignly, "the juggler of Notre Dame?"

The church had come to its feet. Linus was dancing at the door . Children were twisting out of parents' arms.

"One, two, three, four," from the lead guitar. And the song burst out,

"He's got the whole world in His hands,
He's got the whole wide world in His hands,
He's got the whole world in His hands."

The doors were flung wide. A slight young man stood there. A strip of adhesive white against his black forehead, lips parted, his eyes widening, the song lifted:

"He's got Father Jesse Booter in his hands,
He's got Father Jesse Booter in his hands,
He's got Father Jesse Booter in his hands."

The Bishop felt his throat tighten. Agnes flew by him, her apron a banner. Then from the organ loft big plastic sacks began to swing forward on a sort of clothes line trolley till they were poised in place. There was a jerk and they opened as one to spill bright showers of yellow balloons down on the joyous crowd and on the stunned, upturned face of Jesse Booter.

In the sacristy, the Most Rev. Patrick J. Devlin was alone, and that, he thought, was as it should be.

(From *Whisper, Whisper.* Copyright by Doubleday, 1977. Used with permission of the author .)

MARION MARSH BROWN
WANTED MORE BOOKS
FOR YOUNG TEENAGERS

What really started Marion Marsh Brown writing was the dearth of reading material for young high school students.

Brown says that she has always loved to read, and that she "was always scribbling something."

She grew up on a farm near Brownville, so it was natural that she went to nearby Peru State College for her B.A. degree, then on to UNL for her Master's. She did some work on her Ph.D. at the University of Minnesota, but married before it was completed.

Then she taught high school English and discovered "I didn't have any trouble finding reading material for seniors, but I found a gap for younger high school students, and I wanted to fill that gap a little bit."

At her husbamd's suggestion "Why don't you write a book," she started writing in 1949 for young teens, and has continued writing books for all ages until, today, she has sixteen books to her credit.

And she is currently working on a seventeenth.

"Many of my books are historically based," she says. And some of her fiction books are partly autobiographical (*Marnie* and *Prairie Teacher*). The three she collaborated on with Ruth Crone required much historical research.

Of her historical books, she says "I'd do the library research first. Then I'd go to the place the person lived."

"I start with the character first--someone who intrigues me. I live with that person for a while. That's true of every book, whether it is fiction or not."

Brown's career started with feature articles as early as college. Then, "When I was home with a little one, I started writing for Sunday school newspapers. That was my real apprenticeship."

Now she writes about a dozen articles a year.

"There's practically no short story market anymore," she comments. So she writes travel articles ("not travelogues--they are about some relationship that develops"), and some inspirational pieces that are not heavily documented with Scripture.

"I study *Writer's Market*, send out query letters, and I read the publications I'm interested in writing for.

"It's more difficult for me to sell now, because I'm not writing the 'in' thing (sex and violence)."

94

"I do return to markets where I'm known. You get your name associated with certain publishing houses, and they sort of keep you going."

"I've given up a lot to stick to my writing, because it's been important to me," she concludes.

Because *Ladies Home Journal* recently listed Sacajawea as one of the 25 most important women in history, Brown has returned to a lifelong ambition of writing about her, and has begun research.

"When I'm on a book, I write regularly--mornings. "

The Germans are interested in American Indian culture, and her book, *Homeward the Arrow's Flight*, is being considered for translation into German.

"I have to write about something that has value. I can't just write froth," she said. "I want my readers to get something out of it."

From *Marnie*

(Note: Marnie is 14; Twist is 9)

Marnie did wish Twist would finish reading their new book. They had a rule, imposed by their father when Twist first learned to read, that whoever started a book first got to finish it before the other began. Difficult as it was to abide by at times, Marnie knew it was a good rule.

They had received just one book for Christmas, Gene Stratton Porter's *Laddie*. It was inscribed to both of them, and it came from older cousins on their father's side. Daddy had grunted when Twist showed it to him. Marnie knew he was thinking these cousins could well afford a book apiece for her and Twist. But there had also been a box of homemade candy from them, which was so special that she couldn't be resentful over the book. Anyway, *one* book was a real treat.

Suddenly Twist, lying on the floor reading, began to chuckle, then to laugh. "Oh! Oh!" he gasped.

"What's so funny? Tell me," Marnie begged.

"Oh, this--this--" He was off in a paroxysm of laughter. It was contagious, and Marnie started to laugh too.

He tried again. This old gray goose--"

"Yes?" Marnie prompted. "What about the old gray goose?"

"Oh, she was such a goose!"

"Well, what did she do?"

"She ate all this corn, and then--" He was off again. "She drank a whole lot of water, and the corn swelled up-- and--"

"Oh, no!" Marnie cried, anticipating the climax.

"And . . . and she *burst!*" he finally managed.

"Let me read just that part?" Marnie begged.

He handed the book to her and she scanned the page. "I never read such a good book," he said.

(from *Marnie* by Marion Marsh Brown. Used with permission of the author.)

RUTH CRONE SEEKS HOME FOR 'ZANY' STORIES

"I'm clammish about talking about what I'm doing," Ruth Crone whispers in mock confidentiality over a glass of iced tea. "You can talk yourself out of an idea at cocktail parties, or meetings."

"However, I have this unconventional novel looking for a home," she said, that two readers have critiqued and say is "zany. " Crone believes critiquing is important. "But don't give it to a friend. Very few friends are objective. Give it to someone who is objective, intelligent and literate-- preferrably to some one who reads a lot."

"I will say that, with this book, the typography is in keeping with the content. I mesh those two things. It's contemporary. It is considered hilarious and very readable."

Since most of her recent writings have not been books, she was accused of having retired. "I still keep books, I still keep story and article ideas, I still do research. I still write. So how can anyone say I've retired?"

She has retired from two careers: Several years in communications work in Washington, D. C., for the government, followed by 20 years of college teaching. She currently has two book manuscripts "in process."

She keeps daily notes in a book--she has for more than 50 years. These are simple notes, not soul-searching. "I started doing it to find out what I was doing with my time. The notes may include other things--but it still keeps me accountable for my time."

She writes regularly, but "not like going to an office." Her recent articles are personal essays, like one in the *Omaha World-Herald* "*Magazine of the Midlands*" on finding oneself in Kyoto. "This kind of thing is what I like to do best, now."

Crone warns "Never underestimate the intelligence of the reader, nor overestimate his knowledge of the subject."

Crone grew up in Beatrice. She graduated from high school there. During her school years, she decided she would try to read every book in the Beatrice Public Library.

"I didn't succeed. But one book I read that really made an impression on my was *Anne Sullivan Macy* by Nella Brady. It stuck with me."

After graduating from high school, Crone went to Peru State College where she met Marion Marsh (Brown), who was her very young English teacher. After her A.B. degree from Peru, she went to George Washington University for her master's and to New York University for her Ph.D. Then her two careers took her all over the world.

Several years later, Marion Marsh Brown asked her to come up with an idea for a book to write. Crone suggested Anne Sullivan Macy, Helen

Keller's beloved teacher.   After some discussion, they decided to collaborate on it with Brown doing the writing, Crone doing the research, and both doing the editing. Thus, *The Silent Storm*, the fictionalized story of Ms. Sullivan, came out in 1966.

After *The Silent Storm*, Brown and Crone collaborated on two more books: *Willa Cather: The Woman and her Works* in 1970, and *Only one Point of the Compass: Willa Cather in the Northeast* in 1980.

Since the books, Crone has moved from article writing and now does essays.

Her one word of advice to young writers: *Persevere.*

From *Only One Point of the Compass:*
Willa Cather in the Northeast

"A little faster, Claude. A little faster," Willa Cather would say to Claude Gilmore, one of two brothers who ran a taxi service on Grand Manan. It was in the early 1920's, and their cab was a Ford touring car. The roads were narrow and winding, and the Islanders were not a speedy breed. The speedometer on the cab would show thirty.

"A little faster," Miss Cather would say.

A little faster. Forty.

The entourage was enroute to Whale Cove from the pier where the boat from the Mainland had deposited Miss Cather and Miss Lewis. Piles of luggage bounced on the running boards and the top of the cab.

Claude Gilmore pursed his lips. The next time she said it...!

"A little faster, Claude," as she clutched at her wide-brimmed hat which the wind was working to unseat.

"We're going over forty, Miss Cather. That's agin' the law. And your bags're bobbin' like buoys. If you wanna get to Whale Cove with 'em, we'd better go a little slower 'stead of a little faster!"

Later, back with his brother Ray, he complained irritably, "What's the matter with the woman?"

Ray only shook his head. He had had similar expriences with "that writin' woman." After a moment's cogitation, he said, "Reckon she's in a hurry to get to work." The brothers chuckled. To them, being in a hurry to get to work was a joke.

Not so to Willa Cather. Unwittingly, Ray Gilmore had hit upon the truth: Miss Cather was always in a hurry to get to her work. And when she arrived at any of her sanctuaries in the Northeast--Grand Manan, New Brunswick; Jaffrey, New Hampshire; or Northeast Harbor, Maine--she was in a hurry for two reasons: She was eager to get to her work and she was eager to get to the haven which was to afford her quiet and privacy in which to do that work.   Each of these spots, at different times, knew her devotion.   She loved them for their natural beauty, but even more, for the opportunity they afforded her to work undistracted at her writing, for her writing was her life.

(From *Only one Point of the Compass: Willa Cather in the Northeast.* Archer Editions Press. Copyright 1980. Used with permission of the authors.)

FRANCES ALBERTS TOLD
TALES THAT SPREAD

When her pre-school children wanted to hear stories, Frances Alberts created ones so good she almost immediately gained a national reputation as an author of juvenile fiction.

When they learned to read, again it was their mother's books: *New Friends and Neighbors* and *Friends About Us* became classics in the primary textbook market.

As they began reading children's magazines at 9 and 10, their mother published a serial called "Lucky Antlers" in *Children's Activities* and became a regular contributor to *Child Life, The Instructor, Jack and Jill* and other well-known publications for children.

By the time they reached junior high, so did the level of her books. *A Gift for Genghis Khan* was published by McGraw-Hill.

And by the time they were old enough to become interested in the history of Nebraska, Alberts wrote *Sod House Memories.* Volume II is still in print. She recorded 16 summer vacations at their cabin on Lake El Charman in Gibbon with a series of articles in *Focus* magazine and *The Lincoln Star.*

Meanwhile, the children grew up, Alberts became a grandmother, and her writing extended to adult subjects. But half a century after her first works won public and critical acclaim, Alberts is still writing often--and well. She won the Silver Poet Award for 1986 for her poem, "Ancient Sorcery." A recent article, "I Am in Love with Nebraska," appeared in the *The Magazine of the Midlands,* others in the *P.E. O. Record.*

Alberts helped write the history of Adams County Centennial, Vol. I and II, and started the Hastings Writers Group to encourage others to publish their writing.

"I still write every day, and am working on several books at once," she confessed. "You see, once I got started with writing, I just never could stop."

ANCIENT SORCERY

A dream world infinitely aged and old
Lies here beside my real world,
This greenling strip of backyard earth--
For me, here is an ancient sorcery unscrolled.

My heart's toil and heart's thrall, aged and old--
Lie in this dream world.
Time's space apart from backyard earth
And only sorcery blends these worlds.

So as I work with seed and spade and trowel
To bring my flowers to bloom,
My spirit soars this dream world--
With finite happiness, love, infinitely complete.

Used with permission of the author.

I AM IN LOVE WITH NEBRASKA

Nebraska provides food for the intellect, soul and body.

There is a sort of magic, no less, in the sunrises, even more in the moonrise. The stars are so clear, so close, they purely light the night sky even without the moon's help.

There is a satisfying feeling in spring rain pelting down in great drops on my upturned face. I take a pleasure in summer thunder and lightning. A concrete basis for loving affection is built when a friend says to me "Come, walk by the shore into this brilliant sunset," or, "I was concerned about you, did you get home through the storm safely?"

The magnificence of driving through a savage sleet storm with the full forces of nature beautifully unleashed, the pitting of all you have into getting home to your own fire, and the full satisfaction of arriving finally, the winning and the self-confidence that comes, these are worth fighting for. There is here a concern for and a faith in that is not often duplicated.

There are the homey things which make Nebraska beloved to me. A Nebraska home is rich in experience and in love. We live in a changing world, and we live at ever accelerated pace. Yet the things of the heart do not change. Here in Nebraska we hold to the old solid faiths. With our feet securely planted on these, we stand secure in our beliefs. Because of our rich pioneer heritage, we have an inherent claim to these things which our fathers brought to this state.

Historically our state is one of the richest states in the union. All the major settlement trails passed through her. They left behind for us of the Now Generation a rich legacy of thought and way of life.

We stand for a preservation of a way of life, built strongly to begin with on the ideals and values these past generations lived by, and which now continues through generation after generation, as something of heart value.

(*The Magazine of the Midlands*, Aug. 1985. Used with permission of the author.)

WILLIAM COLEMAN GAVE UP MINISTRY FOR WRITING CAREER

William L. Coleman left the Christian ministry 11 years ago to become a full-time, professional inspiration writer. "We had saved up (a little money) and decided to try making a living writing."

He is apparently doing a good job of it. He has an office in downtown Aurora, where he writes. His wife has another office around the corner where she types his manuscripts, does his research, and keeps the accounts.

Coleman has been writing since the fifth grade in Washington, DC, "when a teacher told me, 'That's a good story.'" He realized then and there that there was joy in putting something on paper that people could enjoy. While in high school "I had a teacher who really turned me on to writing. He'd call me in after school and argue with me about what I'd written."

After attending Washington Bible College, Coleman went to seminary in Indiana. His third ministry after graduation brought him to Aurora. By that time he was in his mid-thirties, wanting desperately to devote full time to writing. So he resigned his pastorate eleven years ago, but decided to raise his family in Aurora. "We pretty much starved for three years,"Coleman said, but since then he has had 55 Christian context books published, and 45 are still in print.

"Writing is the only thing I do for a living, " he says. "It says on the board downstairs that I'm William L. Coleman, Author and Educator, but I don't do any teaching any more." "I no longer do articles. You can't make a living doing articles. You get $50 for an article that you could save for a chapter in a book."

Coleman says the three best decisions he made about his writing are to have an office, not to have a telephone in his office, and not typing. About having an office,he says, "I have to go to work. If I stay home, I'm not motivated. I'm not a self-starter." He works from nine to five, but goes home for lunch. His wife works from nine to twelve. His children (ages 17, 19 and 21) have always helped edit his writing, especially the children and teen books. His daughters help with research and typing.

His ideas come from newspapers (" because you know what's current"), and "writing creates ideas. We get three ideas for other books while we're working on this one. We look for a need or a market." Some of his adult books have lots of scripture quotations, but the children's books are just to "enjoy reading, plus one good shot."

When asked for an excerpt to follow this article, Coleman said, "That's hard to do. It's like saying that out of 55 books and 11 years, I have only one thing to say."

From *Chesapeake Charlie and Blackbeard's Treasure*

By early afternoon their plan was beginning to take shape. Charlie had moved his white rowboat off its rack and pulled it to short. Kerry had collected two shovels and a metal detector. They added a small basket of strawberries to their supplies.

"If we get this detector wet, Uncle Ben will have my hide," said Kerry. "I've got to return it before he gets home tomorrow."

"Don't worry. We can buy your uncle a dozen metal detectors when we're done. Put this box near the bow. Without it, we're out of business. These are cookies to give us energy." Charlie handed Kerry an eight-pack of soda.

"No, Throckmorton," Charlie used his roughest voice. The large brown beagle stopped and drooped its head. "You can't come this time." Throckmorton always appeared a little sad, but now he looked as if he might cry. He began to whine softly.

"We might need him," said Kerry. "He makes a tough watchdog."

Throckmorton picked up an orange life jacket in his mouth and stood wagging his tail.

"Sometimes he looks almost human," Charlie said. "All right, but you have to wear the life jacket. The Bay is too deep out toward the middle."

Kerry and Charlie slipped the jacket over Throckmorton's front legs. Charlie then lay on the ground and began to tie the strings. Throckmorton licked Charlie's face.

"Stop that."

"Throckmorton's the only dog I know who would wear a life preserver," Kerry marveled.

(from *Chesapeake Charlie and Blackbeard's Treasure*. Bethany House. Copyright 1981. Used with permission of the author.)

From *Bouncing Back*

Keep Getting Up!

We all know people who seem to get knocked down more than their share. They've had health problems, money trouble, lost love, job setbacks, and termite invasions. Yet each time they shake the dust off, pull in their belts, and come up smiling.

These are the people who face rejection, learn from it, and keep going. What are their secrets? How do they gain their balance? Where do they find the courage to bounce back and climb higher than ever?

Most of us would like to get a handle on rejection. This book is written to help sift out facts from fiction, to help understand what's happening and what we can do about it. It also reminds us that God would like to lend a hand and give us an added bounce.

(From *Bouncing Back*. Harvest House. Copyright 1985. Used with permis - sion of the author.)

CURTIS MADE HISTORY –
THEN WROTE IT

Most histories are written by the victor, says ex-senator and new author Carl T. Curtis. "Mine was by the vanquished."

In his story, *Forty Years Against the Tide*, the Minden native takes pride in being "the minority conservative fighting government give-away programs for 40 years in the U.S. Senate. I was against the school lunch subsidy, Medicare, food stamps, welfare, and what have you," he said.

"We have a terrible deficit frightening all sensible people today. We still have poverty, privation and people making do on less than they should. Spendthrift government programs haven't solved any of those problems."

Curtis wrote *Forty Years* in an effort "to set history straight--correct all the wrongful stories about Richard Nixon, the truth that's never been told before," Curtis said in an interview.

Curtis served under eight presidents and knew 10, he said. "I knew a great many inside stories that had never been published, but needed to be," he said.

Curtis was elected to the Senate in 1938 after growing up as one of seven children of a dryland farmer during the Depression, when Nebraska was part of "the great American desert." The senator considers his greatest achievement creating water programs. There's a Carl T. Curtis Dam and pumping station.

When Curtis couldn't find a book of morning devotionals he liked, he spent an hour every morning before Senate meetings writing his own. *To Remind*, self-published by Service Press in Henderson, was used at Senate prayer breakfasts.

Forty Years required years of research at the Library of Congress, UNL's Love Library, and the State Historical Society. The latter gets the proceeds from sale of the book. The book was written with Regis Courtemanche, an author and professor at Long Island University.

"My next book may well be the history of Nebraska politicans," Curtis said. "I've known every candidate for state office for the last 50 years," he said.

He hopes Nebraska schoolchildren will consider following in his footsteps."If you have a benevolent dictator, he'll look after you and you can sit back complacently," Curtis said. "But in a democratic self-government, nobody else will look after things for you. Only you can do it."

POLITICAL PARTY AND POLITICAL PRINCIPLE

What sort of life will this be? Will America last as a republic in name merely? Will it sink into what Tocqueville called "democratic despotism"? Will an American proletariat grow in numbers and the number of independent Americans steadily shrink? Will the country impoverish itself through ruinous taxation and crushing public debt? Will the morals of most Americans be the morals of Bobby Baker's Carousel Motel? Will American voluntary community be supplanted by involuntary collectivism? Will America continue to resist effectually the "armed doctrine" of the Soviet Union? Will life in this land be worth living? Will Americans, most of them, be permitted to retain even the consolations of religion?

Nobody can answer those questions, the event being in the hand of God. It is forbidden to Christians to endeavor to pry into futurity--to "describe the horoscope, haruscplicate or scry. . .riddle the inevitable with playing cards, fiddle with pentagrams or barbituric acids." For what we call history is no impersonal, inexorable, ineluctable force: history is merely the written record of what has been done in the past. You and we make history. What is to come, you and we will create, or at least we will fulfill unwittingly whatever providence means us to accomplish, our intentions being good. It is not well that we should know the whole future of the Republic, any more than we could endure, any one of us, full knowledge of one's own future. Such a prophecy might work its own fulfillment.

From *Forty Years Against the Tide*, copyright 1986 by Carl T. Curtis and Regis Courtemanche, Regnery Books. All rights reserved. Used with permission of author.

CAN WE COMPREHEND TIME?

A seventh grade history teacher had each member of the class make a chart to illustrate the span of time between events. They used wrapping paper from a roll about 15 inches wide. On the chart each foot represented 100 years. It took a chart 40 feet long to show the time from the ancient Egyptian civilization to the present.

In this 40-foot chart the birth of Christ was right in the middle. Were they to shade that part of the chart which represented the two centuries of the history of America as a nation, the shaded part would be only two-feet long and the unshaded part 38 feet. Leif Ericson's voyage would be marked at a place on the chart 30 feet beyond the beginning of the Egyptian civilization and 10 feet before the present. An individual's life span on the earth of three score years and ten would require less than 9 inches of this 40-foot chart.

Our question for today is, how long would the chart have to be to show the promise to man of life everlasting? In the Scriptures we read, "When. . our body here on earth is torn down, God will have a house in heaven for us to live in, a home he himself made, which will last forever (Corinthians 5:1)."

From *To Remind*, copyright 1982 by Carl T. Curtis, Service Press. All rights reserved. Used with permission of author.

WRITING IS A WAY OF DISCOVERING MEANING FOR MARILYN HELLEBERG

Her remarkable first grade teacher set her first poem to music and had the class memorize the words.

"Of course, I was really hooked on writing, from that moment on," Marilyn Morgan Helleberg, the author of dozens of articles in national magazines and five published books.

Though she now writes six hours every day, Helleberg didn't plan on a writing career. Her first book, *Your Hearing Loss: How to Break the Sound Barrier*, relates to her first chosen profession: speech pathology, which had been her major at the University of Nebraska-Lincoln. The later books, inspirational and spiritual writing, relate to her feelings about being a Christian woman in a world that often appears chaotic and fragmented.

A lover of words, "How could any child who grew up on the *King James Bible* and the *Book of Common Prayer* be less than a lover of language?" Helleberg says she began writing as a way to discover personal meaning in her life.

"Writing forces me to reflect on the events of my life and to seek out the meanings that are just below the surface of everyday incidents," she wrote in a recent article for *The Nebraska Churchman*. "For me, writing is a way of reaching toward wholeness. Sometimes that means allowing myself to be vulnerable, sharing my brokenness in the hope that a reader, by identifying, may reach toward her own kind of wholeness."

Helleberg, a former president of the Nebraska Writers Guild, gained a national reputation from her regular contributions to *Guideposts* magazine. Guideposts Press will publish her fifth book.

But the writing career began in earnest when she went back to Kearney State College for an M.A. degree in English in 1969. A story to a national writer's workshop in New York City won her an all-expense trip to the workshop. She turned every class assignment into a published work.

Helleberg says her favorite kind of article writing is the personal experience type of article, the kind of spiritual quests that she shares in speaking engagements across the country.

"I'm not a real churchy type," Helleberg explains. "But there is a spiritual base which urges me to write, expecially about the personal things. Now I look for meanings just below the surface and, sometimes, can find symbolic meanings in the everyday events that happen to me."

One of the best things writing has done for me as a Christian woman," she writes, "is this: It has convinced me that it's all right to take time just to be."

From *God's Best for You*

(Scheduled for 1987 publication by Guidepost Books, Carmel, N. Y.)

I wasn't ready for her question. We were walking through greening prairie grass along the edge of the Platte River south of Kearney, where we were camped to watch the annual sandhill crane extravaganza. It was the first week in April and about time for the birds to leave the area, for their breeding grounds in the northlands. Maybe it was the thought of those birds and their invisibly guided journey that made Karen ask, with a thirteen-year-old's trust in absolutes, "How can I find out God's purpose for my life, Mom?" I searched for an answer as we stood on the river bank, listening to the sound of the flowing waters punctuated by the wild, echoing calls of the cranes.

Funny about those birds. Every year about the middle of March, it seems as if the sky opens up and rains birds. Some 500,000 cranes spread out over the cornfields, preening themselves, feeding, prancing around in a dance of life that is centuries old yet always fresh and new. For about six weeks they leap and soar and cry at the wind, bringing the grace and the spendor and the pain of poetry into our lives. Then the're gone again, leaving an emptiness out there (and in here) that's a kind of poetry, too.

It's a little like a woman's life: filling up and running over, spilling empty, filling up again . . . each stage a season, each season a poem.

I don't remember how I answered Karen that day, but I sensed a certain childlike wisdom in her question, a rock-solid knowing that said, "I am related to Something bigger than myself, Something more alive than I am, Something older and Something not yet born, that will endure through time. I am not a happening but a has-to-be."

That was fifteen years ago. It's April again. I sit alone by the river now, under the old cottonwood with the hollowed-out trunk where the kids used to play.

Karen and Paul are both married now, John is almost an adult, and I'm a grandma. But this morning the dance of the cranes seems to have erased time. It's as if all of those years of watching them are gathered together into this moment, calling to the child in me. And this wide Nebraska sky, like no other in all the earth, still has on it the marks of my youngest wonder.

BILL RUSH'S REMARKABLE STORY
IS HIS OWN LIFE

When Bill Rush has something to say, he literally hammers his message across loud and clear.

The long stylus attached to his head pecks out letters into words which are then intoned aloud through a mechanical voice. The accent sounds British, but the young author is a native Nebraskan talking about his latest dream: a new book for little kids with a hero who has adventures from a chair on wheels.

"See Dick run. See Jane and Spot run. And see John roll," the words roll our, the ideas popping faster than the pencil-shaped stick can hammer--Rush rushing headlong into a world where others have always feared for him to tread.

Rush was named the Easter Seal Society's Valiant Nebraskan of 1978 and became almost an instant celebrity after the story of how his friend Mark Damke designed a computerized voice was told in *Life* magazine a few years ago. Rush jokes that he became a writer "because I knew a football career or construction work was out."

He has published more than two dozen articles, a media manual, *Write with Dignity*, and a new full-length autobiography to be published by Media Productions, Inc., of Lincoln this fall. All speak to the issue of sensitivity toward people with disabilities. Above all, don't use disabled as a noun, Rush warns his readers.

"I wanted to write sexy novels like Arthur Hailey," he kids with an interviewer. "But when my teacher said to write from experience, I said good-bye to those." Teaching others how to deal with others' disabilities has become a full-time writing mission.

It's other people's misconceptions about so-called handicaps that frustrate this honors graduate student in journalism at the University of Nebraska-Lincoln--not the "inconvenience" of not being able to speak or walk or use his hands.

"Damn, I thought. Here I was graduating from a Big Eight university with distinction--a 3.66 grade point average out of 4.0--and the story in the local paper still reads, 'Cerebral Palsy Victim . . .'"

As he was going up the ramp to receive his diploma, Rush continues in his autobiography, *Journey Out of Silence* , "I remembered Martin Luther King's last speech: 'I have been to the mountain top, and I have seen the promised land . . .'

"I saw my promised land, the people who accepted me. Mom was snapping pictures. Dad was watching proudly. My brothers were applauding. My aunts were crying.

". . . 'We as a people will get there . . .,' King continued. I know that people with disabilities will get to the promised land. All it takes is becoming educated enough to educate others that we're merely humans."

From *Journey Out of Silence*

"WHAT WILL I NEED TO GRADUATE," I asked my J-School advisor, who was carefully going over my record.

"Let's see. You need about 20 hours of nuclear physics and 40 hours of phys ed," my advisor said. "Twenty of which need to be spent at the track. Won't that be fun?"

I nodded and laughed.

"Seriously, you just need three more hours in English, three more hours in one of the social sciences, and three hours in geometry. That's it," my advisor said.

"I CAN'T TAKE GEOMETRY I CAN'T DRAW SHAPES" I spelled.

"Let's go and see the interim dean. Maybe something can be worked out. We could substitute those 20 hours of nuclear physics and 40 hours of phys ed," my advisor said.

The interim dean was merciful. She only made me take three hours of statistics.

"CAN I TAKE IT PASS FAIL" I spelled out.

"Yes you can," she said.

My reasoning for wanting to take the class pass/no pass was simple. I was tired and wanted to coast. I had a nice 3.66 grade point average, which I earned.

As one professor said, "You've proven yourself, so relax this semester. You've earned it."

In March I sent out invitations. This time I sent one to Deanne and her husband.

She joked, "But, Bill, how will we be able to spot you in the crowd? We might miss you."

"DON'T WORRY. I'LL WEAR A RED CARNATION," I shot back.

I also invited Anne Fadiman. To my dismay, she didn't send an acknowledgement. I guessed that things at the Time-Life Building were busy because after her story on Mark and myself had been published, Anne had become a close friend. It was unlike her not to acknowledge the invitation.

In April, 1983, Roger invited me to his wedding. At the reception I told him, "I GUESS THIS IS THE YEAR THAT HELL FREEZES OVER , YOUR MARRYING AND MY GRADUATING HAVE TO FREEZE IT OVER."

"Yeah buddy," Roger said and laughed. "But I always knew you would graduate."

"THANKS FOR HELPING ME . I COULDN'T HAVE DONE IT WITHOUT YOU," I spelled.

"We helped each other, buddy," Roger said.

Three days before graduation, the Affirmative Action Officer called and said that the *Omaha World-Herald* was going to do a story on my graduation. He told me to prepare a statement to save time. He didn't ask me if I wanted to do the interview.

I did what I was told. I didn't see any point in arguing. I had mixed feelings about the publicity. On one hand, my ego loved it. On the other, a lot of college students graduate, but only I was singled out for something unrelated to learning. It didn't seem fair. It seemed akin to those barbaric circus sideshows--no matter how distant.

I told the reporter my feelings, and he said that he would take them into account.

Then he asked me a startling question: "Do you feel that your degree has the same value as the others?"

"WHAT DO YOU MEAN?" I spelled, somewhat taken aback.

"I mean do you feel that the professors gave you the grades out of pity," the reporter said. It was the first time the question had been raised.

I answered it honestly. "I DON'T KNOW. I JUST DID THE ASSIGNMENTS. ASK MY PROFESSORS."

"I did, and the chairman of the News-Ed department said that you earned everything you got," the reporter said after consulting his notes. I breathed a sigh of relief. Then the photographer with the reporter took several pictures of me in my cap and gown.

A couple of days before the big day, Mom informed me that my graduation party would be delayed a week because she would be too tired to have it immediately following the ceremony.

The graduation rehearsal was short, but not sweet. The head marshal informed me that I wasn't going to be in the processional or the recessional, rather I would be seated before the processional and leave the floor after the recessional. He also told me that I would be pushed up the ramp to the stage where I would get my degree. The tone of his voice made it clear that his decision was final.

I wanted to be in the processional, in the recessional, and my electric wheelchair, but graduation was only 16 hours away. I didn't want to complicate the home stretch.

When I got home, I was still angry. I was certain that the head marshal was wrong, but I didn't know what to do about it. Then, I discovered that my door didn't lock when I left. I took a quick inventory: Computer, printer, carnation, my special phone. . . Wait a second. Carnation? I didn't have a carnation when I left. I wheeled closer to the flower to read the scribbled note. "We wanted to make sure we could pick you out tomorrow. Love ya, Deanne."

I laughed and cried at once.

Soon, Roger and another male friend showed up to take me to meet Mark. When we got to the lounge, I was glad to see that Mark had a date and wished that I had a date. His date had her back to the door, but even from the back I could tell that she was good-looking. "Good for you, friend," I thought.

I was preparing for an introduction, but got a warm hug. It was Anne Fadiman.

"You didn't really think I would miss your graduation, did you?" Anne said softly, still hugging me.

(From *Journey Out of Silence*. Copyright 1986 by William Rush, Media Productions. Used with permission of the author.)

DIRECTORY

I. POETS

John Stevens Berry, Box 4554, 2650 No. 48th St., Lincoln, 68504
Darkness of Snow. San Luis Obispo, CA. Solo Press, 1973

Elinor L. Brown, 113 W. Elm St., Ceresco, 68017
Morning Glories. Ceresco, Midwest Press, 1983

Susan Strayer Deal, 1721 Harwood, Lincoln, 68502
No Moving Parts. Boise, ID. Ahsahta Press, 1980
The Dark Is a Door. Boise, ID. Ahsahta Press, 1984

Musetta Gilman, 5340 Colby St., Lincoln, 68504
Graffiti. Madison, WI. F.A.S. Publishing, 1973.
Trails. Detroit, MI. Harlo Press, 1986

Linnea Johnson, 1746 So. 14th, Lincoln, 68502
The Chicago Home. Cambridge, MA. Alice James Books, 1986

William Kloefkorn, 2502 No. 63rd St., Lincoln, 68507
Honeymoon. Kansas City, MO. BkMk Press, 1982
Voyages to the Inland Sea (with Hale Chatfield). La Crosse, WI.
Center For Contemporary Poetry, 1977
Alvin Turner As Farmer. Garland. Windflower Press, 1977
Uncertain the Final Run To Winter. Garland. Windflower Press,
1977
Cottonwood County (with Ted Kooser). Garland. Windflower
Press, 1980
Not Such a Bad Place to Be. Port Townsend, WA. Copper
Canyon Press, 1980
Platte Valley Homestead. Lincoln. Platte Valley Press
ludi jr. Lincoln. Platte Valley Press
Collecting for the Wichita Beacon. Lincoln. Platte Valley Press
Houses and Beyond. Lincoln. Platte Valley Press
A Life Like Mine. Lincoln. Platte Valley Press
Let the Dance Begin. (chapbook). Pittsford, NY. State Street
Press

Ted Kooser, Rt. 1, Box 10, Garland, 68360
Official Entry Blank. Lincoln. University of Nebraska Press, 1969
A Local Habitation and a Name. San Luis Obispo, CA. Solo
Press, 1974
Not Coming to Be Barked At. Milwaukee, WI. Pentagram Press,
1976
Sure Signs. Pittsburgh, PA. University of Pittsburgh Press, 1985
One World at a Time. Pittsburgh, PA. University of Pittsburgh
Press, 1985
Blizzard Voices, St. Paul, MN. Bieler Press, 1985

Greg Kuzma, Crete, 68333
   Village Journal. Crete. Best Cellar Press, 1978
   For My Brother. Omaha. Abattoir Editions, 1978
   Everyday Life. Peoria, IL. Spoon River Poetry Press, 1983
   A Horse of a Different Color. Los Angeles, CA. Illuminati, 1983
   Of China and of Greece. New York, NY. Sun, 1984

Calvin A. Miller, 11929 Woolworth Ave., Omaha 68144
   The Singer. Downers Grove, IL. Intervarsity Press, 1975
   The Singer Trilogy. Downers Grove, IL. Intervarsity Press 1980

Hilda Raz, 201 Andrews Hall, University of Nebraska, Lincoln, 68588
   Poetry Editor, *Prairie Schooner.* Lincoln. University of Nebraska

Robert Richter, Rte. 1, Box 293, Ogallala, 69153
   Windfall Journal. Markleeville, CA. Jelm Mountain Press, 1980

Richard Schanou, 1010 2nd Ave., Aurora, 68818
   Editor, *The Nebraska Counselor*, Aurora

Roy Scheele, 2022 So. 25th St., Lincoln, 68502
   Accompanied. Crete. Best Cellar Press, 1974
   Noticing. Lincoln. Three Sheets Press, 1979
   Pointing Out the Sky. Ord. Sandhills Press, 1984 (Now available
       at Nebraska Bookstore)
   Poems for the Dead, Pebble 23. Crete. Best Cellar Press, 1984
   Pocket Poems. New York, NY. Bradbury Press, 1985

Donald Welch, Kearney State College, Dept. of English, Kearney, 68849
   Deadhorse Table, Garland. Windflower Press, 1975
   Handwork, Kearney, Kearney State College Press, 1978
   The Rarer Game, Kearney, Kearney State College Press, 1980
   On Common Ground. North Platte. Sandhills Press, 1983
   The Keeper of Miniature Deer, Juniper Press, 1986

Kathleene West, 204 Andrews Hall, University of Nebraska-Lincoln 68588
   Plainswoman: Her First Hundred Years. North Platte. Sandhills
       Press, 1985
   Water Witching. Port Townsend, WA. Copper Canyon Press, 1984

II. LITERARY, SOCIAL, AND NATURAL HISTORY

Frances Jacobs Alberts, 734 No. 2nd Ave., Hastings, 68901
  Sod House Memories, Vol. II, Henderson. Service Press, 1961

Peggy Benjamin, 1524 Coventry Lane, Grand Island, 68801
  Years to Share. Henderson. Service Press, 1986

Mildred Bennett, 329 No. Cedar, Red Cloud, 68970
  The World of Willa Cather. Lincoln. University of NE Press, 1985
  Early Stories of Willa Cather. New York, NY. Dodd Mead & Co.,
    1957
  Editor, "The Willa Cather Pioneer Memorial Newsletter." Red
    Cloud. The WCPM Society

John Stevens Berry, Box 4554, 2650 No. 48th St., Lincoln, 68504
  Those Gallant Men: On Trial in Vietnam. Novato, CA. Presidio
    Press, 1984

Elinor L. Brown, 113 W. Elm St., Ceresco, 68017
  History of Lancaster County, Then and Now. Ceresco. Midwest
    Publishing, 1971
  *Architectural Wonder of the World: Nebraska's State Capitol
    Building ,* Lincoln Yearbook, 1978

Marion Marsh Brown, 11619 Burt St., Apt. R21, Omaha, 68154
  The Brownville Story. Lincoln. Nebraska State Historical Society,
    1974
  Homeward the Arrow's Flight, Nashville, TN. Abingdon Press,
    1980
  Only One Point of the Compass (with Ruth Crone) Lynnville, TN.
    Archer, 1980
  Dreamcatcher: The Life of John Neihardt (with Jane Leech)
    Nashville, TN. Abingdon Press, 1983

Carl T. Curtis, Apt. 104W, 1300 G St., Lincoln, 68508
  Forty Years Against the Tide. Lake Bluff, IL. Regnery Gateway,
    Inc., 1986

James Martin Davis, 500 Continental Bldg., Omaha,68102
  Raids. Springfield, IL. Charles Thomas, 1982

Belle Fenley Edwards, P.O. Box 1032, North Platte, 69101
  Heart Full of Horses. San Antonio, TX. Naylor Co., 1975

Bill Ganzel, 1125 So. 21st St., Lincoln, 68502
>*Legacies of the Depression on the Great Plains.* Produced by
>NETCHE. Lincoln. UNL, Ne.ETV, 1983.
>*Riders on the Storm* (TV Documentary)
>*Of Dust Bowl Descent.* Lincoln. University of Nebraska Press,
>1984

Musetta Gilman, 5340 Colby, Lincoln, 68504
>*Pump on the Prairie.* Detroit, MI. Harlo Press, 1981

William Holland, 1650 Farnam St., Omaha, 68102
>*Let a Soldier Die.* New York. Delacorte, 1984.

John Janovy, Jr., 400 Sycamore Drive, Lincoln, 68510
>*Keith County Journal.* New York, NY. St. Martin's Press, 1980
>*Yellowlegs.* New York, NY. St. Martin's Press, 1980
>*Back in Keith County.* Lincoln. University of Nebraska Press,
>1983
>*On Becoming A Biologist.* New York, NY. Harper and Row, 1985
>*Fields of Friendly Strife.* New York, NY. Viking, 1986

Paul A. Johnsgard, 7341 Holdrege, Lincoln, 68505
>*Song of the North Wind: The Snow Goose.* New York, NY.
>Doubleday, 1974
>*Those of the Gray Wind: The Sandhill Cranes.* New York, NY. St.
>Martin's Press, 1981

Orleatha Kellogg, 235 W. 20th St., Fremont, 68025
>*Bloom on the Land.· A Prairie Pioneer Experience.* Henderson:
>Service Press, 1982.

Maxine Kessinger, P.O. Box 512, Elkhorn, 68022
>*Sing the Praises.* Lyons. Clark Printing Co., 1976

Wayne Lee, Lamar, 69035
>*Trails of the Smoky Hill.* Caldwell, ID. Caxton Printers, Ltd.

Robert Manley, 2515 Pioneer Blvd., Grand Island, 68801
>*Nebraska: Our Pioneer Heritage.* Lincoln. Media Productions &
>Marketing, 1981

James L. McKee, 3425 Otoe, Lincoln, 68506
>*Lincoln: A Photographic History.* Lincoln. J & L Lee, 1980
>*Lincoln, the Prairie Capital.* Woodland Hills, CA. Windsor Press,
>1984

Elaine Nielsen, Box 599, Ogallala, 69153
  Ogallala: A Century on the Trail. Marcelene, MO. Walsworth
    Press, 1984

Margaret Stines Nielsen, 403 W. 23rd, Kearney, 68847
  The Life and Times of Doc Nielsen. Lincoln. Word Services, 1979
  Tales of Buffalo County. Kearney. Buffalo County Historical
    Society, 1981, 1984

Margaret Virginia Ott, 116 So. 9th St., Nebraska City, 68410
  Man with a Million Ideas (with Gloria Swanson). Minneapolis, MN.
    Lerner Publications, 1981

Wallace C. Peterson, Dept. of Economics, University of Nebraska, Lincoln,
    68588
  Our Overloaded Economy. Armonk, NY. M.E. Sharpe, 1982

Caroline Sandoz Pifer, Gordon, 69343
  Victorie and Other Stories by Mari Sandoz. Crawford, NE
    Crawford Press, 1986

Robert T. Reilly, 9110 No. 52nd Ave., Omaha, 68152
  Rebels in the Shadows. Pittsburgh, PA. University of Pittsburgh
    Press, 1962
  Irish Saints. New York, NY. Crown Publishers, Inc., 1964

Robert Richter, Rte. 1, Box 293, Ogallala, 69153
  Plainscape: A Portrait of Perkins County. Grant. Perkins County
    Historical Society, 1987

Sue Rosowski, Department of English, Andrews Hall, University of
    Nebraska, Lincoln, 68588
  The Voyage Perilous. Lincoln. University of Nebraska Press,
    1986

Barbara Tupper, Inavale, 68905
  County Fair. Inavale. Wild Clover Books, 1985

Ruth Van Ackeren, 801 S. 52nd St. #612, Omaha,68106
  Bartlett Richards: Nebraska Sandhills Cattleman. Lincoln. Ne.
    State Historical Society, 1980

Nellie Snyder Yost, 1505 W. D St., North Platte, 69101
  Before Today. O'Neill. Holt County Historical Society, 1976
  Buffalo Bill, His Family, Friends, Fame, Failures and Fortunes.
    Athens, OH. Ohio University Press, 1979
  Back Trail of an Old Cowboy. Lincoln. University of Nebraska
    Press,1983
  Keep On Keeping On. North Platte. Nellie Snyder Yost
  No Time on My Hands. Lincoln. University of Nebraska Press,
    1986

III. FOLKLORE, STORYTELLERS, HUMORISTS

Teresa Bloomingdale, 2044 So. 86th Ave., Omaha, 68124
    I Should Have Seen It Coming When the Rabbit Died. New York,
        NY. Doubleday, 1979
    Up the Family Tree. New York, NY. Doubleday, 1980
    Murphy Must Have Been a Mother. New York, NY., Doubleday,
        1980
    Life is What Happens When You're Making Other Plans. New
        York, NY. Doubleday, 1983
    Sense and Momsense. New York, NY. Doubleday, 1984

Reba Pierce Cunningham, 1524 Trelawney Dr., Lincoln, 68512
    Cowboys, Cooks, and Catastrophes. Stillwater, OK, Barbed Wire
        Press, 1985

Gladys Douglass, 6315 O St., Lincoln, 68510
    Oh, Grandma, You're Kidding. Lincoln. J & L Lee,1983

Duane Hutchinson, 3445 Touzalin Ave., Lincoln, 68507
    Doc Graham: Sandhills Doctor. Lincoln. Foundation Books, 1971
    Images of Mary. Lincoln. Foundation Books, 1971
    Exon: Biography of a Governor. Lincoln. Foundation Books,
    1973
    Savidge Brothers: Sandhills Aviators. Lincoln. Foundation
    Books, 1982
    Storytelling Tips. Lincoln. Foundation Books, 1985

Shirley Lueth, 1409 9th St., Aurora 68818
    Bubble, Bubble, Toil and Trouble. New York, NY. Morrow, 1984
    I Didn't Plan to be a Witch. New York, NY. Avon, 1981
    Watch Out!! I'm Peeking In Your Window. Aurora. Lueth House
        Publishing Co., 1986

Roger Welsch, 3511 Mohawk, Lincoln, 68510
    Omaha Tribal Myths & Trickster Tales. Athens, OH: Ohio
        University Press, 1981
    Shingling the Fog and Other Plains Lies. Lincoln. U of Ne Press,
        1980
    Mister, You Got Yourself a Horse. Lincoln. U of Ne Press, 1980
    Treasury of Nebraska Pioneer Folklore. Lincoln. U of Ne Press,
        1984
    Inside Lincoln: Lincoln. Plain's Heritage Press, 1983
    You Know You're a Nebraskan. Lincoln. Plain's Heritage Press,
        1985
    You Know You're a Husker. Lincoln. Plain's Heritage Press, 1986

IV. NOVELISTS

Barbara Bonham, Franklin 68939 or 2901 Paddock Plza., Omaha, 68124
    Passion's Price. New York, NY. Berkeley Jove, 1982
    Dance of Desire. New York, NY. Berkeley Jove, 1978
    Green Willow. New York, NY. Berkeley Jove, 1982
    Bittersweet. New York, NY. Berkeley Jove, 1982

Howard M. Crilly, 849 Washington St., Superior, 68978
    The Night the Opera House Burned. Bryn Mawr, PA. Dorrance &
        Co., 1984.

Marnie Ellingson, 3411 So. 94th Ave., Omaha, 68124
    Double Folly. New York, NY. Dell, 1980
    Unwilling Bride. New York, NY. Dell, 1980
    Jessica Windom. New York, NY. Dell, 1980
    Counterfeit Honeymoon. New York, NY. Dell, 1980
    The Mistress of Langfort Court. New York, NY. Dell, 1982
    The Wicked Marquis. New York, NY. Walker, 1982
    Dolly Blanchard's Fortune. New York, NY. Walker, 1983

Ruth Richert Jones, 3320 Pine, Omaha, 68105
    My Heart to Give. (pseudonym, Carmen Leigh). Eugene, OR.
        Harvest House, 1984

Catherine Kidwell, 643 So. 11th St., Lincoln, 68508
    Dear Stranger. New York, NY. Warner Books, 1983, 1984

Wayne Lee, Lamar, 69035
    Putnam's Ranch War. New York, NY. Thomas Bouregy, 1982
    Barbed Wire War. New York, NY. Thomas Bouregy, 1983
    The Violent Trail. New York, NY. Thomas Bouregy, 1984
    White Butte Guns. New York, NY. Thomas Bouregy, 1984

Judith Nelson, 4121 Starr, Lincoln, 68505
    The Merry Chase. New York, NY. Warner Books, 1985

Beth Schrempp, 700 So. 89th St., Omaha, 68114
    Whisper, Whisper (pseudonym Katherine Court). Garden City, NY.
        Doubleday, 1977

V. CHILDREN AND YOUNG ADULTS

Karren Boehr, RFD, Box 37, Henderson, 68371
>*Ants in the Sugarbowl.* St. Louis, MO. Concordia Publishing House, 1986

Barbara Bonham, Franklin, 68939 or 2901 Paddock Plza, Omaha, 68124
>*Challenge of the Prairie.* New York, NY. Bobbs-Merrill, 1965
>*Crisis at Fort Laramie.* Des Moines, IA. Meredith Press, 1967
>*Willa Cather.* Radnor, PA. Chilton, 1970
>*To Secure the Blessings of Liberty.* Hawthorn, 1970
>*Bonanza Heroes of the Midwest.* Western Publishing Co, 1970

Marion Marsh Brown, 11619 Burt, Apt. R21, Omaha, 68154
>*Marnie.* Philadelphia, PA. Westminster Press, 1971
>*The Pauper Prince.* New York, NY. Crescent, 1973

Ruth Crone, 1938 So. 39th St., Omaha, 68105
>*The Silent Storm.* (With Marion Marsh Brown) Grand Rapids, MI. Baker Book House, 1985

William L. Coleman, 1115 9th St., Aurora, 68818
>*Earning Your Wings.* Minneapolis, MN. Bethany House, 1984
>*The Great Date Wait.* Minneapolis, MN. Bethany House, 1982
>*Animals That Show and Tell.* Minneapolis, MN. Bethany House, 1982
>*Counting Stars.* Minneapolis, MN. Bethany House, 1985
>*Chesapeake Charlie and the Bay Bank Robbers.* Minneapolis, MN. Bethany House, 1980
>*Chesapeake Charlie and Blackbeard's Treasure.* Minneapolis, MN. Bethany House, 1981
>*Getting Ready for Our New Baby.* Minneapolis, MN. Bethany House, 1984
>*The Good Night Book.* Minneapolis, MN. Bethany House, 1979
>*On Your Mark.* Minneapolis, MN. Bethany House, 1979
>*The Warm Hug Book.* Minneapolis, MN. Bethany House, 1985
>*Courageous Christians.* Minneapolis, MN. Bethany House, 1982
>*Jesus, My Forever Friend.* Minneapolis, MN. Bethany House, 1981
>*Who, What, When, Where Book about the Bible.* Minneapolis, MN. Bethany House, 1980
>*Who, What, When, Where Busy Book.* Minneapolis, MN. Bethany House, 1984
>*How, Why, When, Where Book about the Bible* (4 volumes). Minneapolis, MN. Bethany House, 1985
>*Bernie Smithwick and the Super Red Ball.* Minneapolis, MN. Bethany House, 1984
>*Bernie Smithwick and the Purple Shoestring.* Minneapolis, MN. Bethany House, 1984
>*The Palestine Trumpet.* (4 volumes) Minneapolis, MN. Bethany House, 1985

Josephine Frisbie, 122 So. 39th., #1203, Omaha, 68131
and Gunnar Horn, 5006 Walnut, Omaha 68106
>*Murder in the Old Mill.* Omaha. Wright Printing Co., 1979
>*Murder in the Museum.* Omaha. Wright Printing Co.,1980
>*Murder in the Churchyard.* Omaha. Wright Printing Co.,1981
>*Murder on Maple Street.* Omaha. Wright Printing Co.,1982

Tom Frye, 6110 Kearney, Lincoln, 68507
>*Scratchin' on the Eight Ball.* Lincoln. Media Productions and
>Marketing,1982

Dorothy Hintz, Rte. 1, Box 63, Belvidere, 68315
>*Treasure in the Deep Blue Sea.* Belvidere. Bell Publishing, 1981

Paul A. Johnsgard, 7341 Holdrege, Lincoln, 68505
>*Dragons and Unicorns: A Natural History.* New York, NY. St.
>Martin's Press, 1982
>*Prairie Children: Mountain Dreams.* Lincoln. Media Productions
>and Marketing, 1985

Dorothy Kripke, 11611 Burt, Omaha, 68154
>*Let's Talk About the Jewish Holidays.* Middle Village, NY.
>Jonathan David, 1982

Robert T. Reilly, 9110 No. 52nd Ave., Omaha, 68152
>*Red Hugh, Prince of Donegal.* New York, NY. Farrar, Straus and
>Giroux, 1966
>(Also made into a Walt Disney movie)

VI. MOTIVATION AND INSPIRATION

Elinor L. Brown, 113 W. Elm St., Ceresco, 68017
Where Are You Going? Ceresco. Midwest Publishing, 1976

William L. Coleman, 1115 9th St., Aurora, 68818
You Can Be Creative. Eugene, OR. Harvest House, 1983
Peter. Eugene, OR. Harvest House, 1982
Bouncing Back. Eugene, OR. Harvest House, 1985
The Newlywed Book. Minneapolis, MN. Bethany House, 1985

Grant G. Gard, P.O. Box 34579 N.W. Sta., Omaha, 68134
Don't Talk About It, Do It. Omaha. Grant G. Gard, 1974
The Art of Confident Public Speaking. Englewood Cliffs, NJ.
Prentice-Hall, 1985
Championship Selling. Englewood Cliffs, NJ. Prentice-Hall, 1984

Bernice Hogan Hanks, 6228 Oak Hills Plaza, Omaha, 68137
My Grandmother Died (children's). Nashville, TN. Abingdon, 1983

Marilyn Helleberg, 1702 W. 35th St., Kearney, 68847
A Guide to Christian Meditation. New York, NY. Walker and Co.,
1985
Where Soul and Spirit Meet. Nashville, TN. Abingdon, 1986
God's Best for You. New York, NY. Guideposts Books, 1987
Your Hearing Loss. Chicago, IL. Nelson-Hall, 1980

Orleatha Kellogg, 235 W. 20th St., Fremont, 68025
Holiday Nonsense and Common Sense. Fremont. Fremont
Printing Co.,1985

Marilyn Marsh, 2102 So. 106th St., Omaha, 68124
How to Write for Christian Magazines. Nashville, TN. Broadman
Press,1985

Fr. Joseph McGloin, S.J., Creighton University, Omaha, 68131
I'll Die Laughing. Chicago, IL. Loyola, 1985

Tom Osborne, University of Ne. Lincoln Athletic Dept., Lincoln, 68588
More Than Winning. Nashville, TN. Nelson Press, 1985

William Rush, 817 C St., Apt. 1, Lincoln, 68508
Journey Out of Silence. Lincoln. Media Productions. 1986

Editors' note: Authors in this section are listed in *Books in Print* . To find additional authors in your area who publish in anthologies, periodicals, produce self-published works, or who may have extra copies of their books no longer in print, write the Nebraska Writers Guild Clearinghouse, 318 E.12th St., North Platte, 69101

INDEX

* Especially good with elementary school children.